Teaching *Romeo and Juliet*

D1560465

Teaching *Romeo and Juliet*

A Differentiated Approach

Delia DeCourcy

Lyn Fairchild
Duke University

Robin Follet
Cary Academy, Cary, North Carolina

National Council of Teachers of English
1111 W. Kenyon Road, Urbana, Illinois 61801-1096

Staff Editor: Bonny Graham

Interior Design: Doug Burnett

Cover Design: Jody A. Boles

Cover Image: iStockphoto.com/Martin Krasilnikov

Text art courtesy of Robin Follet.

NCTE Stock Number: 01124

It is the policy of NCTE in its journals and other publications to provide a forum for the open discussion of ideas concerning the content and the teaching of English and the language arts. Publicity accorded to any particular point of view does not imply endorsement by the Executive Committee, the Board of Directors, or the membership at large, except in announcements of policy, where such endorsement is clearly specified.

Every effort has been made to provide current URLs and email addresses, but because of the rapidly changing nature of the Web, some sites and addresses may no longer be accessible.

Library of Congress Cataloging-in-Publication Data

DeCourcy, Delia, 1973–
    Teaching Romeo and Juliet : a differentiated approach / Delia DeCourcy, Lyn Fairchild, Robin Follet.
        p. cm.
    Includes bibliographical references.
    ISBN 978-0-8141-0112-4 ((pbk))
    1. Shakespeare, William, 1564–1616. Romeo and Juliet. 2. Shakespeare, William, 1564–1616—Study and teaching. 3. Drama—Study and teaching—United States. 4. Drama in education. I. Fairchild, Lyn, 1968–   II. Follet, Robin, 1971–   III. Title.
PR2831.D35 2007
822.3'3—dc22

2007015089

Contents

Acknowledgments

In many ways, this project began for me when I started teaching *Romeo and Juliet* in 1999. Each year I grew to understand and love the play more. I must thank my eighth-grade students for being such good sports about being my guinea pigs. They provided me with the feedback that improved my methods for teaching Shakespeare year after year. Colleague, mentor, and friend Carol Morgan deserves prolonged applause for being a wonderful listening ear, brainstorming partner, and intellectual partner in crime. Her encouragement, support, and feedback helped make me the teacher I am. Thank you to Lyn for spearheading this project and making it a reality. Her vision, intelligence, creativity, and drive are enviable! Thank you to Robin for his tremendous insight, careful attention to detail, and unfailing calm. This paragraph would not be complete without an acknowledgment of my parents. Their appreciation of literature and support of my early theatrical career were the seeds of my love for Shakespeare.

Delia DeCourcy

This book is dedicated to the many people who have made the writing of this book possible. Carol Tomlinson, Cindy Strickland, and the dedicated instructors at the Summer Institute for Academic Diversity at the University of Virginia's Curry School of Education helped me grasp the spirit and structure of differentiated instruction. Enthusiastic students over the years who brought the Bard to life on makeshift stages have made teaching and performing Shakespeare a delight: I'll never forget the "Athenians" of Los Altos High School; the "Veronese" of Stanford Middle School; and the island and tempest-tossed Umstead Park dwellers and the Mafioso Macbeths of Cary Academy.

I would also like to thank my high school English teacher Angela Connor, who first let me play the Nurse in ninth-grade English and who made me love Macbeth mulling over yesterday and tomorrow. Years later, Los Altos High School colleague Sarah Mayper taught me how to direct a Shakespearean script and bring its beauty to life, while mentors Roma Hammel and Celia Baron showed me the skill of teaching "Skills," "College prep," and "Honors" kids while never limiting a student to a label. Thanks go to Brian Cooper for reviewing this manuscript and for animated and inspirational sessions of reflective thinking about teaching. Throughout everything, my parents Stephen and Katherine Fairchild have been my biggest cheerleaders; I thank them for keeping Shakespeare on the shelf and taking me to Stratford-upon-Avon. My sister Antonia Fairchild inspires me with her gift of creating a Forest of Arden wherever she alights. My husband Greg Hawks gives me his constant love and support as a fellow artist who understands the need to create.

Finally, I thank Robin Follet and Delia DeCourcy for taking this journey with me. They are true "Shakespeers" who know the play's the thing—for everyone!

Lyn Fairchild

Thank you to my family, for their love; to my teachers, for their perseverance; and to my coauthors, for their friendship, their advice, and their gift of a nifty moniker.

Robin Follet

Introduction

Welcome, Gentle Reader!

We've pictured you while designing these units: a Shakespeare aficionado trying heroically to address diverse student readiness levels, interests, and learning styles while trying to inspire passion and wonder for the Bard's work. In other words, you want to differentiate—to develop units that meet the diverse needs of your diverse students—but time flies from you.

The good news is, you probably already employ strategies that fit perfectly within the tall order that differentiation sometimes appears to be, strategies such as multiple-intelligence activities, Paideia discussion, project-based learning, complex-instruction group work, and backwards planning for enduring understandings and essential questions. The curriculum detailed in this book offers you a broad buffet of differentiated options as well as a template of sample lessons to help you develop a schedule of activities that organizes this variety of diverse approaches.

What's Inside

- As a refresher (or an introduction), Chapter 1 of *Teaching* Romeo and Juliet: *A Differentiated Approach* provides a brief overview of differentiated instruction.

- In Chapter 2, we offer an in-depth exploration of act 1 of *Romeo and Juliet*. The lessons, beginning with the Prologue, enable all students to grasp the language, the plot, and the themes of the play. By focusing on key scenes from each act, the curriculum focuses your class on common goals and a common experience. Lesson pacing moves from whole-class discussions to small-group or individual projects, and returns to whole-group interactions, in which students can reflect together on themes. Carefully plotted lesson activities provide differentiation by readiness, interest, and learning profile. Scaffolded reading activities in the form of reproducible handouts ensure that all students practice close reading at their readiness level while meeting local, state, and national standards. Before, throughout, and after the unit, students demonstrate their knowledge and abilities through formal and informal assessments; with this knowledge, you will be able to stretch them within their zones of proximal development, whether you're teaching a student who is struggling with basic vocabulary comprehension or a pupil aching to discuss the use of embedded sonnets.

Chapter 2 ends with act 1 skill strand projects that allow students to follow their interests while studying the play. Cinematography, creative writing, Socratic discussions, drama—these skill strands all offer every student a chance to become an expert in an area of preference while studying Shakespeare's work.

- The subsequent four chapters—one chapter per act—follow a similar pattern.

- Appendixes provide additional information on grading in a differentiated classroom, Web sources on Shakespeare, and some suggested readings.

It's likely you know how diverse the audience was that first saw Shakepeare's plays at the Globe. With your creativity, rigor, compassion, and persistence, you can ensure that your heterogeneous classes enjoy Shakespeare's work as much as the Elizabethans once did. We hope that our book will serve you well, allowing you to mix the joy of Shakespeare's work with the pleasure of teaching.

1 Some Basic Information about Differentiation

A Primer on Differentiating the Bard's Works:
We'll measure them a measure

What's different about differentiation? Why differentiate the Bard's plays? Here are some philosophical principles that underpin differentiated instruction of Shakespeare's classic works:

- All students should have access to Shakespeare.

- Higher achievement is possible for all students. A teacher can harness pre-, mid-, and postassessment to identify a student's prior, current, and ultimate knowledge and then help a student evolve beyond the initial diagnosis.

- A Shakespearean play should be discussed, analyzed, interpreted, acted, and owned rather than covered. Learning occurs when the student makes meaning—i.e., constructs rather than receives understanding.

- Implementing a variety of pedagogical approaches maximizes student retention and increases understanding, thus addressing fundamental competencies demanded of students on standardized assessments.

- Rituals and routines allow the teacher to establish expectations, check for understanding, and maximize student performance, while a diverse offering of activities allows for engagement, excitement, and student choice. Both approaches are essential to effective teaching practice.

- All students should have a chance for success within a unit of study. Tiered assignments address a student's readiness level and allow students to make progress within their zone of proximal development.

- All students should feel part of a community of learners. Whole-class tiered and mixed-readiness assignments address students' needs for belonging as well as interpersonal learning styles.

The challenge of differentiation is not only in the skills required to manage an active classroom, lead a good discussion, or inspire reluctant students, but also in choosing well from the large buffet of pedagogical choices. Here are some tips to help you relax while trying new teaching strategies:

- Don't let the range of choices overwhelm you. Pick those that suit your students and that also spark your interest, since you too have preferred interests and a learning profile and work best in your areas of passion. By the same token, you should challenge yourself within your zone of proximal development, which is the learning curve in which you feel yourself stretching, but not to the breaking point.

- Which leads to our next point: you can't change everything at once. Try something new this year and study the experience you and your students had. Modify the activity for use the next year, and then add a new activity or approach to your repertoire every year.

- Be a teacher-researcher. Differentiated instruction encourages you to take good notes and even keep a reflective journal in which you can jot reactions and impressions. Talk shop with colleagues who teach the same subject. Gather your data on student progress and reactions to activities, grab a moment's reflection, and make notes for next year's activities.

A Teacher's Glossary for Differentiated Instruction: Words, words, words

Differentiated instruction includes the best practices of educational research: those teaching strategies that respond to differences in students' readiness level, interests, and learning styles; preparation of students to meet national and state standards; and development of a learning community united by themes, content, and skills. The following terms, drawn from current research, we will use frequently throughout lessons:

> *Advanced student*: A student whose knowledge and skills are more sophisticated than grade-level peers and who performs one or more levels above grade level. Throughout this book, we will use ADV to refer to advanced students.

Anchoring activities: Brief activities rooted in content and skill or thematic understanding that students can complete as warm-ups or culminating class activities, or as personal choice assignments (for example, journal entries).

Bloom's taxonomy: Levels of abstraction for questioning and activities, beginning with knowledge, moving to comprehension, to application, to analysis, to synthesis, to evaluation. See *tiered questions*.

Close readers: Questions, tables, and outlines provided in handout form to assist reading comprehension and interpretation of literature. Throughout the book, we will use *CR* to designate these exercises.

Compacting: A specialized learning program for advanced students who have demonstrated through assessments the knowledge of grade-level content and skill proficiency and potential to learn with more independence. Compacting students work on enrichment or accelerated studies during class and at home, occasionally rejoining the larger group.

Interest: A method of differentiation that uses student areas of expertise and curiosity.

Jigsaw activity: Group work in which students complete one task in small groups and then reassemble in a second group to share content and skills gained during the first group task.

Learning style: The mode through which a student best absorbs, engages with, and constructs knowledge and skill. Categories include the kinesthetic, aural, visual, verbal, interpersonal, intrapersonal, and other learning styles.

Mixed-readiness group: Activities or assignments in which students are clustered by interest, learning profile, and/or choice and complete a complex task designed for a variety of interests and readiness levels. Throughout the book, we will use *MR* to designate mixed-readiness activities.

Novice student: A student who performs below grade expectations and demonstrates a need for content and skills remediation. *NOV* will refer to novice students.

On-target student: A student who performs at or close to grade expectations for mastering content and skills. *OT* will refer to on-target students.

Readiness: A method of differentiation that organizes students according to their ability to complete assignments below, at, or above grade-level expectations.

Skill strand activities: Activities and projects that ask students to demonstrate proficiencies such as dramatic performance skills, Socratic discussion skills, creative writing skills, or cinematic analysis skills. These activities also meet student interests to motivate learning.

State standards: Reading comprehension and writing skill competencies that students must demonstrate by the end of the school year.

Tiered questions: Questions differentiated by readiness level for tiered-readiness assignments. Use Bloom's taxonomy to create questions at different levels of abstraction. Note: While NOV and even OT learners who struggle with reading need to focus on knowledge and comprehension questions, they also should be given chances to try analytical and evaluative questions with enough support.

Tiered readiness: Activities or assignments in which students are clustered by readiness level to complete a task designed for a certain level of content and skill understanding. *TR* will refer to tiered-readiness activities.

Whole-class activity: A multisensory and/or multiple-intelligence activity designed to inspire, challenge, and motivate all students while emphasizing grade-level content and skills. Whole-class activities frame units and unify a class after students have explored content and skills with TR or MR assignments. Throughout the book, we will use WCA to designate whole-class activities.

Student Observations: Reading o'er the volume of young Paris' face

Differentiated instruction encourages a teacher to make observations throughout a unit about student readiness, interests, and learning style. Just as every student is both unique and atypical within any of the three categories of NOV, OT, and ADV, each student will also follow some patterns and trends. Each student has potential to stretch beyond his or her initial designation. Observe a range of students as you begin to teach this unit. Select students who have shown NOV, OT, and ADV patterns in your last unit. Ask yourself:

1. What are each student's strengths in reading comprehension and writing? (Consult past assessments and recall your observations.)

2. With what skills does this student struggle? At what grade level does this student perform? What should be the focus concerning content and skill remediation?

3. What are each student's interests? (Consult the Bardometer, other interest inventories, and parent feedback, observations, and interviews.)

4. Which of the student's interests can I harness to expand learning opportunities?

5. What are each student's strengths in terms of learning style? (Consult learning style inventories and use parent feedback, observations, and interviews.)

6. What learning styles can I harness to expand learning opportunities?

7. What role does this student play during class?

8. What are my predictions about how this student will approach Shakespeare?

Handout: The Bardometer, a Student Interest Inventory

Name _____ Period _____

1. My favorite activities, hobbies, and pastimes are _____ .
2. On the weekends or in the summers, the best thing I've ever done
   is _____ .
3. A subject, person, place, or thing I'd like to know more about is
   _____ .
4. A topic I could share information about for several minutes is
   _____ .
5. A goal I have is _____ .

Circle all your favorite approaches for learning below (you can circle just one verb in a list or the whole statement):

I like writing, performing, or directing a skit/screenplay.

I like writing a story, novel, poem, or song.

I like designing/making costumes, sets, or props.

I like planning, composing, performing music.

I like participating in or leading a discussion or a debate.

I like painting a picture, drawing/sketching/doodling, cartooning.

I like making models, dioramas, sculptures, prints, or collages, etc.

I like solving problems and finding solutions.

I like looking for patterns using numbers or words.

I like watching films and analyzing actors, action, shots, special effects, or sound/music effects.

Circle the themes of most interest to you:

LOVE & MARRIAGE   REBELLION   FATE   IDENTITY

HASTE VERSUS SLOWNESS   NIGHT VERSUS DAY   MASKS

DICHOTOMY & PARADOX

Reading Shakespeare: A most courteous exposition

In an ideal world, each student we teach would read every word of a Shakespeare play and savor it. While we pause to sigh that this is not our reality, we might resuscitate our spirits with a solution: that less is more. If we can guarantee that our students savor some words well, then we can worry less about whether they are reading all of them.

Our TR assignments are designed so that students can tackle reading comprehension questions at their readiness level during both homework and in-class activities. These assignments target different quantities of text and different levels of Bloom's taxonomy depending on student readiness, but they always focus on a specific text selection, which for NOV and OT students is usually not an entire scene. Our philosophy is that coverage is not as important as comprehension of key scenes; gaps in the narrative can be filled by a combination of class discussion, performance, and focused reading assignments for homework.

How Much Should Students Read on Their Own?

To plan nightly reading assignments, determine how much time you think it will take an NOV, an OT, and an ADV student to read a certain number of pages per night. If reading five pages is going to take an NOV student more than an hour, consider asking students to try reading just one passage (10–30 lines) independently without supplements (in other words, just the help that our close readers offer) and then using supplements for the remainder of the nightly reading. Likewise, focus other students' independent reading on passages rather than pages, drawing their attention to the most important sections.

Please note that all passages from Shakespeare's text are quoted from the Oxford edition.

What Are Good Supplementary Reading Resources?

NOV students can use the SparkNotes edition of *Romeo and Juliet* (Crowther) from the No Fear Shakespeare series as their backup resource. The right-hand side supplies traditional text and the left-hand side provides a line-by-line translation. OT students can use the online printouts or purchasable editions of Charles and Mary Lamb's *Tales from Shakespeare* or Warren King's *No Sweat Shakespeare* as their backup resource, both written in short story or novella styles.

ADV students can use a dictionary and a Shakespeare glossary. *Shakespeare's Words* by David and Ben Crystal provides multiple definitions of words, conjugation of Elizabethan verb forms, and explication of allusions.

What Should Students Be Doing While They Read Independently?

When students are not prompted by our close readers to read certain passages closely, you can provide other guidelines to encourage good reading habits with other sections of the play:

- *Marking the text*: As recommended by Mortimer J. Adler in his famous essay "How to Mark a Book," encourage students to actively read by marking up a text. Consider copying key passages as homework handouts so that students can write on them with pen, pencil, or highlighters, or giving students different-colored sticky notes for marking their school-owned copies. Each day's class can begin with students sharing their discoveries and questions about last night's reading.

- *Writing about the text*: Dialectical journals (also known as double-entry journals, a two-column note-taking table) encourage students to dialogue with the text. Students copy key quotations in the left-hand column and then in the right-hand column ask questions, identify key plot points, analyze character, discover elegant diction, predict consequences, connect to other scenes, and make personal connections.

Remember that *Romeo and Juliet* is many students' first introduction to Shakespeare. Reading just enough well rather than racing through too much poorly will reap rewards for your students.

2 Act 1: Lessons, Handouts, and Assessments

Act 1 is a crucial opportunity for you to diagnose student abilities while providing a fun and inspiring introduction to the Bard. Several prefatory activities in this unit allow you to gauge your students' readiness and interests as you model close reading and encourage maximum comprehension. We recommend that you proceed slowly through act 1 to ensure student understanding. Investing dollar time early on to get students acquainted with the language always pays off and prevents your spending penny time every day thereafter trying to catch students up on translation skills while calming their frustration. Thus we recommend you spend at least three class periods reviewing the Prologue. You can give certain skill strand assignments, particularly the creative writing assignments, for homework during those evenings (these assignments can be found at the end of the chapter). Note also that for act 1, we provide close readers (CRs)—close reading activities—for every scene, whereas from act 2 on, we provide only one per act. You can therefore pick up speed in acts 2 through 5. You can also use our CRs as templates to develop close reading activities for other scenes.

Lessons typically run fifty minutes in length and can be combined to become a ninety-minute series of activities. Optional activities are also included, such as mini-lessons, journals, performances, and theme discussions, which increase a lesson's length by twenty to thirty minutes (also see the end of the chapter for Socratic seminar discussion questions and useful mini-lessons). Handouts are labeled by lesson letter and number and appear at the end of each lesson. Many of the handouts include a glossary of words that some students may need help with; the glossed words are boldfaced in the text. Finally, another abbreviation you'll find used often in the following lessons is AS, which means that an activity is suitable for all students.

After each lesson, we recommend reflecting on your students' progress. Consider using the following questions. Diagnosis of student skill should not be permanent but instead organic and ongoing.

- Do activities meet content and skill standards?
- Do readiness levels of tiered activities seem appropriate?

- Do interest-based and multiple-intelligence activities meet students' interests?
- What needs adjustment as I approach the next lesson?

Act 1, Prologue

Lesson PRO.a: Translate It

Student Content and Skill Understandings

- Prepare to read and engage with a Shakespeare text: summarize, define, predict, translate, highlight. (AS)

Materials and Handouts

- PRO.a.1: The Prologue handout
- PRO.a.2: Complete Thought Checklist handout
- PRO.a.3: Act 1 Journals handout
- Dictionaries and glossaries

Activities

STEP 1. WCA: Mini-Lesson/MR Groups on Finding the Complete Thought (25 minutes)

1. Explain to students how reading older literature like Shakespeare's plays is detective work. We begin with what we already know—such as vocabulary that we share with the Elizabethans—and seek further knowledge and skill to crack the mystery. Take time to explain the differences between close reading and skimming and how active reading means questioning and reacting throughout the play.

2. Distribute copies of handout PRO.a.1: The Prologue, which is the text of the Prologue with guidelines for close reading. Ask students to read the Prologue aloud slowly with you, putting a dot above words they already know. Ask for a dot count from various students.

3. Ask students to read this excerpt once again as a class, and this time underline any words that rhyme. Explain how to indicate rhyming patterns with an a, b, c, or d rhyme scheme.

4. Distribute The Search for the Complete Thought Checklist (PRO.a.2) handout, which helps students note the parts of speech in Shakespeare's verse as well as his meaning.

5. MR groups: Ask students to work in pairs or triads using the checklist to find the simple sentence hidden in the Shakespeare one.

6. WCA: Ask students to report back their simple sentences and model their sentences using visual aids on the Prologue lines 1–4 that you have posted. Ask them to explain how they determined that *households* and *break* function as the subject and verb respectively while *we*, *lay*, and *blood* do not.

STEP 2. MR Groups: Further Practice on Finding Shakespeare's Complete Thought (25 minutes)

1. Distribute copies of the Prologue to MR groups. Provide cards and highlighters if necessary. Tell students that the complete thoughts will not be elegant but instead "baby sentences" of SUBJECT + VERB. They do not need to translate every word perfectly.

2. Ask students to translate lines 5–8 of the Prologue into simple sentences using the steps on The Search for the Complete Thought Checklist. Note: if you have highlighters, markers, and colored index cards available, students can write their subjects and verbs on yellow and green cards respectively or in yellow and green marker on white cards. Green symbolizes action for verbs ("go," or the green light) and yellow symbolizes the subject for nouns (the sun, the center and source of a sentence's action).

3. Ask students to share their translations and hold up cards as they present. Tell them that they should always look for this complete thought whenever they read Shakespeare.

4. Ask the whole class to read aloud the Prologue with you at a faster speed and place dots over words they now know.

5. MR groups: Ask pairs or triads to answer this question with a sample sentence: *If you were saying this sen-*

tence from the Prologue using a modern English grammatical arrangement from today, how would it read? Use all or most of the words, add no more than two words if you must, and do not change any of the vocabulary into simpler words. Think about what phrases modify which words. Consider this sample modern sentence for lines 1–4: *Both alike in dignity, two households in fair Verona, where we lay our scene, break from ancient grudge to new mutiny. There civil blood makes civil hands unclean.* Another approach is to have students cut up their Prologue handouts and move words and phrases around like magnetic poetry until they achieve a sample modern sentence.

Epilogue: Suggested Homework

Have students complete journal entries and/or begin creative writing skill strand activities. Note that journal entries also function as excellent ten-minute anchoring activities to focus students at the beginning of class.

Notes on Differentiation

1. These translation exercises prepare students for the pretest (PRO.b.1: Prior Knowledge Survey handout), which requires that the students translate the remainder of the Prologue.

2. If many of your students struggle with grammar, take the whole class through each step of The Search for the Complete Thought Checklist during the mini-lesson and review the grammatical functions of those words not in the simple sentence. If necessary, review terms such as *subject*, *verb*, and *independent* versus *dependent clause*, as well as the meanings of words such as *fair*, *mutiny*, *civil*, and *toil*, before students move into MR groups.

3. ADV students who may soon be compacting can translate lines from the Prince's speech in act 1 if they are already familiar with the Prologue, or present information on the structure of a sonnet to the class. These students should already have indicated to you a strong knowledge of the play. See the PRO.d.2: So You'd Like to Compact Shakespeare handout (see page 39).

Handout PRO.a.1: The Prologue

The Most Excellent and Lamentable Tragedy of Romeo and Juliet

THE PROLOGUE

[*Enter* CHORUS.]

CHORUS. Two households, both alike in dignity

(In fair Verona, where we lay our scene)

From ancient grudge break to new mutiny,

Where civil blood makes civil hands unclean.

From forth the fatal loins of these two foes

A pair of star-cross'd lovers take their life,

Whose misadventur'd piteous overthrows

Doth with their death bury their parents' strife.

The fearful passage of their death-mark'd love,

And the continuance of their parents' rage,

Which but their children's end nought could remove,

Is now the two hours' traffic of our stage;

The which if you with patient ears attend,

What here shall miss, our toil shall strive to mend.

Directions for close reading:

1. Place a dot above any words whose meanings you already know.
2. Underline any words that rhyme.
3. Find and circle the nouns that are subjects of each action being performed.
4. Find and box the verbs that indicate the subjects' actions.

Teaching Romeo and Juliet: *A Differentiated Approach* by Delia DeCourcy, Lyn Fairchild, and Robin Follet © 2007 NCTE.

Handout PRO.a.2:
The Search for the Complete Thought Checklist

Inside every Shakespeare sentence is a simple one: a subject and a verb that make a complete thought. Let's do some detective work to discover Shakespeare's essential meaning.

1. Look at the first four lines of the Prologue and read them aloud up to the first period.

2. Discuss the definitions of any unfamiliar words, using a dictionary or your partner(s)' prior knowledge. If there is a disagreement on meaning, check with the teacher.

3. Circle all the nouns you see that might be subjects.

4. Box all the verbs you see that might be the main verb—the action the subject is completing.

5. Discuss with your partners these questions as you search for the complete thought. Discard certain verbs and nouns that do not express the main idea.

   a. Which verb expresses an action or links an idea?

   b. Which noun performs that action or is linked to other ideas?

   c. Draw an arrow between the subject and the verb.

6. Write out the simple sentence you have created: circles + boxes.

Remember, a (sentence) [is] a complete thought. (It) [must] [contain] a subject and a verb.

Teaching Romeo and Juliet: *A Differentiated Approach* by Delia DeCourcy, Lyn Fairchild, and Robin Follet © 2007 NCTE.

Handout PRO.a.3: Act 1 Journals

Themes of Act 1: Rebellion, Lust, Dichotomy, and Paradox

Directions:

1. Write at least 250 words in response to your chosen question.
2. Write without stopping for at least ten minutes. Do not censor your thoughts but write what first comes to mind.
3. Give specific examples such as **anecdotes** or **allusions**.
4. Do not worry about the organization, spelling, grammar, or punctuation of your paragraphs. While it is important to use all those **conventions**, they should not freeze up your writing! Let the flow of your thoughts **dictate** the order of your words.
5. Most important, let this journal reflect your thoughts, questions, and opinions.

Journal Prompts:

1. *Rebellion*: What rules do you struggle to follow? Why? What are the consequences when you do follow the rules? What are the consequences when you don't? What rules do you see others struggling to follow? Why? What consequences have they experienced?
2. *Lust*: How is lust viewed by our society? In what situations is lust approved of? In what situations is it **condemned**?
3. *Dichotomy & Paradox*: How can a person or a thing **exhibit** opposite characteristics **simultaneously**? (For example, can you feel both love and hate for one person? How and why?)
4. **CHALLENGE QUESTION:** What do these three themes have in common? Make some connections.

Glossary:

allusions: references to events and characters in other works of literature, film, media, and the arts

anecdotes: brief stories from personal experience or brief stories you have read

condemned: criticized and determined to be bad

conventions: rules

dictate: determine, decide

exhibit: show

simultaneously: at the same time

Teaching Romeo and Juliet: *A Differentiated Approach* by Delia DeCourcy, Lyn Fairchild, and Robin Follet © 2007 NCTE.

Lesson PRO.b: Translate It

Student Content and Skill Understandings

- Prepare to read and engage with a Shakespeare text: summarize, define, predict, translate, highlight. (AS)

Materials and Handouts

- PRO.b.1: Prior Knowledge Survey handout
- PRO.a.3: Act 1 Journals handout (see page 17)
- Video or DVD versions of the Franco Zeffirelli and Baz Luhrmann films
- Mini-Lesson 1: The Shakespearean Sonnet (see page 148)

Activities

STEP 1. WCA: Prior Knowledge Survey (30 minutes)

1. As a review, ask students to turn to a partner and summarize lines 1–8 of the Prologue to each other. Call on random partners to present their summaries.

2. Distribute the Prior Knowledge Survey, which is a pretest of students' prior knowledge and skill using the Prologue's text. Explain that credit is based on effort; even guessing at synonyms for single words is better than leaving lines completely blank. Encourage students not to worry and to try their best so that you can develop the best lesson plans to meet their needs.

STEP 2. WCA: Feedback on Prior Knowledge Survey (5 minutes)

1. Ask students what strategies they used to complete the Prior Knowledge Survey.

STEP 3. WCA: Project Explanation and Mini-Lesson on the Prologue (15 minutes)

1. OPTIONAL: Present a brief mini-lesson on the Prologue and its sonnet structure (see page 148 for Mini-lesson 1: The Shakespearean Sonnet and its student handout, Notes on the Shakespearean Sonnet, page 150) or give students a brief explanation of the purpose of the Prologue in a Shakespeare drama. Some suggested facts to share: (a) The pro-

logue was a convention of Elizabethan theater. It was a speech spoken by one actor who summarized the play, introduced the theme, and calmed the audience before the play began. (b) The Prologue also set the tone, the emotional mood of the play. (c) When the Prologue actor said "Verona" (Italy), the audience assumed that the Italian characters would be passionate, strong-tempered, and loyal to family honor. Mentioning an Italian city carried the same weight as an allusion today to *The Godfather* movies or the TV series *The Sopranos*. (d) Elizabethan theater depended on listening, not seeing—no fancy sets or special effects—so actors described settings for the audience. (e) The stage consisted of a bare area in open air, with the audience on all three sides. Actors told the audience if it was day or night since the play was always performed in daylight. Ask students if they have ever been in a play where there was a prologue or a narrator who introduced the play and even explained various characters' actions or the upcoming plot. Ask a TR question (ADV because it is evaluative) about what the benefits and drawbacks are to having a prologue start the action.

2. OPTIONAL: Show the Zeffirelli and Luhrmann versions of the Prologue and ask TR questions.

   a. OT: How do visual effects or sound effects chosen by the filmmakers match the words?

   b. ADV: Which film illustrates the tone of the Prologue the best? Why?

3. Preview the Present the Prologue! activity to be started tomorrow (see page 26).

Epilogue: Suggested Homework

Have students complete journal entries and/or begin creative writing skill strand activities.

Notes on Differentiation

1. When you pose TR questions to everyone in a WCA, note who steps up to answer. The question might be labeled

ADV, but an NOV student may soar with it.

2. Depending on your assessment of student readiness as a whole, vary the amount of time allowed for the Prior Knowledge Survey.

3. Consider not giving a pretest to a class in which most student reading levels are extremely low and well documented. Instead, move to lesson PRO.c. You may want to spend a whole period translating the Prologue together, using the Tips for Tackling the Language handout (see page 25).

4. Sort your students' surveys to determine future TR groups. NOV readers: students who can't list more than one to two plot events, are reluctant to translate more than a few words, and/or mistranslate most if not all of the text; OT readers: students who know a few plot events and/or are able to translate some lines with 30–50 percent or more accuracy; and ADV readers: students who claim to have read or acted a significant portion of the play and/or can translate 60 percent or more accurately. Vary these percentages as needed depending on your students' readiness levels and age.

5. Since you know your students best, determine what constitutes a meaningful effort for each child in order to give participation credit on these surveys. Students should not be penalized with grades if they made a sincere effort for their readiness level.

6. To gather private and informal feedback on their first experience with translating Shakespeare, consider stopping a few students who represent varying readiness levels. You can continue this approach for a variety of activities to keep up to date on the range of readiness levels and the experiences of your students.

Handout PRO.b.1: Prior Knowledge Survey
of Romeo and Juliet

Student Name _____ Period _____

Please DO NOT WORRY about whether you know these answers. Try your best to fill in as much as you can. By answering honestly, you help me assess what you will need in order to understand and enjoy this play. Stop whenever time is called.

I. Past Experience: Have you read, seen the play or movies of, or ever acted in *Romeo and Juliet*? If you answer yes, please elaborate in the space provided.

❏ Yes _____

❏ No

II. Plot Knowledge: List as many events as you know occur in the story of *Romeo and Juliet*.

1. _____
2. _____
3. _____
4. _____
5. _____
6. _____
7. _____
8. _____
9. _____
10. _____

III. Language Translation: Write your translation beneath each line for the last six lines of the Prologue. You do not have to translate word for word. Or, if you know few words, write synonyms for the words you do know.

The Most Excellent and Lamentable Tragedy of Romeo and Juliet

THE PROLOGUE
Remember seeing the first eight lines before?

> Two households, both alike in dignity
> (In fair Verona, where we lay our scene)
> From ancient grudge break to new mutiny,
> Where civil blood makes civil hands unclean.
> From forth the fatal loins of these two foes
> A pair of star-cross'd lovers take their life,
> Whose misadventur'd piteous overthrows
> Doth with their death bury their parents' strife.

Now you translate the following:

CHORUS.   *(continued)*

The fearful passage of their death-mark'd love,

_____

And the continuance of their parents' rage,

_____

Which but their children's end nought could remove,

_____

Is now the two hours' traffic of our stage;

_____

The which if you with patient ears attend,

_____

What here shall miss, our toil shall strive to mend.

_____

Lesson PRO.c: Present It

Student Content and Skill Understandings

- Prepare to read and engage with a Shakespeare text: summarize, define, predict, translate, highlight. (AS)

Materials and Handouts

- PRO.c.1: Tips for Tackling the Language handout
- PRO.c.2: Present the Prologue! handouts
- PRO.c.3: Notes on the Sonnet handout (found at the end of the chapter)
- Markers/crayons/art supplies; poster board or butcher paper; percussive objects such as pots, boxes, cans, spoons, rattles, etc.
- OPTIONAL. Electronic slideshow software, such as PowerPoint
- Dictionaries and Shakespeare glossary
- Franco Zeffirelli's and Baz Luhrmann's film versions of *Romeo and Juliet*

Activities

STEP 1. WCA: Review of Skills (15 minutes)

1. Ask students to share the strategies that worked for translating the last six lines of the Prologue on their own. Remind students that detective-like and slow close reading will be the approach for now until their comfort level increases.

2. Ask the class to read the Prologue aloud slowly with you.

3. Distribute and review the Tips for Tackling the Language handout, a list of translation and reading strategies they will use throughout the unit. Lead the class in translating lines 9–14 of the Prologue by modeling the strategies from the handout.

4. OPTIONAL: Present a mini-lesson on the Prologue and its sonnet structure.

STEP 2. MR: Present the Prologue! Preparation (35 minutes)

1. Distribute and review the Present the Prologue! handout for the activity that asks students to use their preferred learning style to present eight lines of the Prologue. Explain that this activity is another preassessment. Explain the importance of both the Director role and group consensus.

2. Allow students to select from four groups differentiated by learning style or interest.

3. Give students the rest of the period to translate the eight lines of the Prologue and prepare their presentations. The logical-mathematical group(s) may need assistance with explanations of iambic pentameter, alliteration, and/or sonnet rhyme scheme, though their observations of letters, syllables, and rhyme can be enough. Observe when groups effectively use reading strategies on the Tips for Tackling the Language handout.

Notes on Differentiation

1. An ADV student might present information during mini-lesson time on the structure of the sonnet and/or present a recitation of the Prologue.

2. Consider giving the Bardometer (see Chapter 1) before this lesson and dividing students into interest groups based on their responses to that survey.

3. Note that the verbal-linguistic activity is essentially an advanced skill activity.

4. If your class has several NOV students who did poorly on the pretest, spend more time on review of skills in the Tips for Tackling the Language handout.

5. Use observations during group work plus the Prior Knowledge Survey to obtain data to help you divide students for future TR activities.

Handout PRO.c.1: Tips for Tackling the Language

Use the following eight skills whenever you encounter a Shakespeare passage for the first time:

1. **Getting the Structure:** Where does the complete thought end? Where are the subject and the verb? Remember: Shakespeare sometimes puts the verb before the subject.

2. **Sounding It Out:** What modern word does this word sound like?

3. **Building on What We Know:** Which words that I do understand help me understand those I don't?

4. **Skipping for Now:** Which unknown words will I **table** until I understand the main idea of this passage?

5. **Guessing the Meaning:** What are my guesses about word definitions?

6. **Consulting the Experts:** What do the dictionary, glossary, or text references say the definition is?

7. **Getting the Joke:** What were the jokes of the time? What were the **puns** about?

8. **Getting the Point:** What are the key words in this line(s), the nouns and the verbs? What main idea(s) do they express? What theme(s)?

Whenever you visit Elizabethan England, always use the BARD It! strategy: before you ask your teacher, BARD It!

Break open your book

Ask each other for *help*, not answers.

Read the references, and then read the text again.

Don't forget the dictionary.

Glossary:
puns: plays on words using multiple meanings of a word or similar-sounding words
table: put aside, postpone, hold for later

Teaching Romeo and Juliet: *A Differentiated Approach* by Delia DeCourcy, Lyn Fairchild, and Robin Follet © 2007 NCTE.

Handout PRO.c.2: Present the Prologue!

Your Task: Use your preferred learning style to introduce our class to the meaning and tone (the feeling or mood) of Shakespeare's Prologue to *Romeo and Juliet*.

Directions:

1. Form a group of three to five people based on one of the intelligences described below. Choose a Director who will ask everyone for ideas and ask for **consensus** before **implementing** decisions.

2. Translate the Prologue by writing your best understanding of *at least eight lines*, using the Tips for Tackling the Language handout. You may use the play and its text references as well as dictionaries and glossaries.

3. Follow the instructions for your intelligence group to create your presentation. You will be graded on (a) correct translation of content; (b) full member participation; (c) creative presentation; and d) substantive explanation.

Glossary:
consensus: an agreement that everyone can live with, in which everyone gets a little bit of their way; a compromise
implementing: making

Group 1: Visual-Spatial

Task: Draw **literal** pictures and **symbolic** and decorative words to represent the most important parts of the Prologue. Hold these up at appropriate moments while reading or reciting the **excerpt** you chose from the Prologue.

Preparation Questions:

1. Which eight lines do you want to present and why?

2. Do you understand most if not all of the eight lines you want to present?

3. What words are most important and should be represented with pictures? How do you know? (Choose at least one for every two lines.)

4. What kind of pictures should you use for certain words—literal or symbolic? Why? How can you emphasize certain words by making them decorative?

---

5. What is the tone of the Prologue as a whole? Can all your images fit into some kind of **unified** design?

6. What is the best way to organize your presentation?

    a. Will you read as a group or divide lines?

    b. Who will hold up the pictures and when?

    c. Who will explain why we created these visual aids?

Glossary:

excerpt: section, part

literal: realistic (if the Prologue mentions an apple, draw an apple)

symbolic: figurative, representing an idea and carrying broader meanings and associations (if the Prologue mentions love, you draw a heart)

unified: connected, together as one whole, following the same idea or theme

---

Group 2: Bodily-Kinesthetic

Task: Use your bodies to represent the most important lines of the Prologue with pantomime, freeze-frame, gesture, and other movements, performing the **excerpt** of the Prologue like a chorus.

Preparation Questions:

1. Which eight lines do you want to present and why?

2. Do you understand most if not all of the eight lines you want to present?

3. What words and phrases are most important and should be represented with movements? (Choose at least one per line.)

4. What is the tone of the Prologue as a whole? Can all your movements fit into some kind of **unified choreography**?

5. What is the best way to organize your presentation?

    a. Who will read and who will move?

    b. How will you move creatively?

    c. Where will each person stand?

    d. When should people perform the motions?

    e. How can we use the whole performance space creatively?

continued on next page

Glossary:
choreography: moves
excerpt: section, part
unified: connected, together as one whole, following the same idea or theme

Group 3: Logical-Mathematical

Task: Use the syllables, repetition, rhyme, and other patterns in the Prologue to present the most important lines of the Prologue like a chorus with **percussive** instruments, or present the **excerpt** of the Prologue like a teacher's lecture with a pointer or electronic slideshow to demonstrate the patterns.

Preparation Questions:

1. Which eight lines do you want to present and why? (Note: You may want to use all fourteen lines to fully see the patterns.)

2. Do you understand most if not all of the eight lines you want to present?

3. Place a mark over every syllable or word that your group thinks should be emphasized. What words and phrases are the subjects and main verbs and therefore need to be emphasized? What words are rhymed? Stress all of those. Read the lines aloud and emphasize these words as you state them, and change your marks as needed so that the stresses fall where a speaker would naturally place the emphasis.

4. Count the number of words per line. Do you see a pattern?

5. Identify the rhyme scheme. Do you see a pattern?

6. Do you see any initial consonant sounds repeated in a series of words, or do you see any vowel sounds repeated within a line?

7. Do you see a pattern of certain syllables emphasized from line to line (stresses falling on the first or second syllable each time)?

8. Do you see any other patterns in these lines? Does any pattern get broken?

9. What is the best way to organize your presentation?

    a. Will you beat out the rhythms you find with percussion or read aloud the emphasized syllables while pointing to a poster?

b. Who will explain which pattern(s), and what will you say about the choice of words that are emphasized by these patterns?

Glossary:
excerpt: section, part
percussive: rhythmic, drumlike

Group 4: Verbal-Linguistic

Task: Identify the **connotations** of key words to predict key themes established by the Prologue, and present the Prologue like a teacher's lecture. Create a poster for your lecture that highlights words you will explicate and/ or illustrate.

Preparation Questions:

1. Which eight lines do you want to present and why? (Note: You may want to use all fourteen lines to fully see the themes.)

2. Do you understand all fourteen lines of the Prologue?

3. What words and phrases are most important in each line? Which of these key nouns, verbs, and adjectives have interesting connotations? (Choose at least one per line.)

4. What themes do these words establish?

5. Are there different thematic sections to the Prologue? Does the mood of the Prologue change? Where? Why?

6. What types of plot events might illustrate such themes? What types of characters might illustrate such themes?

7. What is the best way to organize your presentation? Who will read and who will explain?

Glossary:
connotations: associations, suggestions, and implications of a word beyond its dictionary definition

Teaching Romeo and Juliet: *A Differentiated Approach* by Delia DeCourcy, Lyn Fairchild, and Robin Follet © 2007 NCTE.

Handout PRO.c.2: Present the Prologue! continued . . .

The Most Excellent and Lamentable Tragedy of Romeo and Juliet

THE PROLOGUE

[*Enter* CHORUS.]

CHORUS.   Two households, both alike in dignity

_____

(In fair Verona, where we lay our scene)

_____

From ancient grudge break to new mutiny,

_____

Where civil blood makes civil hands unclean.

_____

From forth the fatal loins of these two foes

_____

A pair of star-cross'd lovers take their life,

_____

Whose misadventur'd piteous overthrows

_____

Doth with their death bury their parents' strife.

_____

The fearful passage of their death-mark'd love,

_____

And the continuance of their parents' rage,

_____

Which but their children's end nought could remove,

_____

Is now the two hours' traffic of our stage;

_____

The which if you with patient ears attend,

_____

What here shall miss, our toil shall strive to mend.

_____

Teaching Romeo and Juliet: *A Differentiated Approach* by Delia DeCourcy, Lyn Fairchild, and Robin Follet © 2007 NCTE.

Lesson PRO.d: Present It

Student Content and Skill Understandings

- Prepare to read and engage with a Shakespeare text: summarize, define, predict, translate, highlight. (AS)

Materials and Handouts

- Materials and handouts from lesson PRO.c.
- PRO.d.1: Very Punny handout
- PRO.d.2: So You'd Like to Compact Shakespeare handout

Activities

STEP 1. MR: Preparing the Prologue (25 minutes)

1. Continue preparatory work started during lesson PRO.c.

STEP 2. WCA: Presenting the Prologue (25 minutes)

1. Ask each group to present to the whole class, ending with group(s) 4. Encourage students to compliment one another's performances and to comment on how the different intelligences illuminate different aspects of a text.

2. Ask students if they still have any questions about translations, and clarify any serious misunderstandings of the language by asking students to volunteer other translations.

Epilogue: Suggested Homework: ADV

Ask students who you think may qualify for compacting to see you for a brief conference. Before they begin with project proposals, consider asking them to complete the Very Punny handout.

Notes on Differentiation

1. This assessment adds to evidence you are gathering on student readiness levels for translating Shakespeare's text and student learning styles. Students who did not comprehend the Prologue in the previous lesson will be pick-

ing up new vocabulary and reading strategies while using their preferred learning style and/or by watching, listening, and discussing the presentations. The results of these lessons can also determine TR groupings for act 1 lessons.

2. Very Punny and its companion scene can be an alternative presentation assignment for an advanced student.

3. Steps to the Compacting Process:

   a. Determine what grade-level content and skill objectives all students must meet by the end of this Shakespeare unit. Survey local, state, and national English standards, along with the content and skill objectives that preface all of these lessons. Which content and skill objectives must students demonstrate in order to have grade-level understandings? What constitutes grade-level proficiency in meeting these objectives? Which students should have the curriculum compacted because they can more quickly meet or have already met the objectives for this unit?

   b. Offer assessments—pretests—at the beginning of the unit in which advanced students can demonstrate their prior knowledge and skill in reading and writing. We suggest that you use the acts 1–5 quizzes that assess basic plot knowledge, as well as the Post-Play Poll (see pages 271–72). Students who make a score of a high B or better on these assessments should be able to "compact out." Other justifications for compacting can include achievement and aptitude tests on which students have placed above the 85th percentile, though some districts prefer that scores be 90th percentile and above (see your school's definition of *gifted*). Because Shakespeare's language is different from the language used on standardized tests, also use your own pretests that expose the students to Shakespeare's text. A pretest can be modeled after the Prior Knowledge Survey using any passages from the play. If you create one, be sure to provide a brief plot summary to give the excerpt context.

c. Determine what "compacting out" means for each student who qualifies and develop a learning contract for each that reflects those learning objectives. You can look ahead in your state and local expectations for grade-level proficiencies and provide challenges at an eighth-grade level to your seventh grader, or tenth-grade level to your ninth grader, and so forth. Note that not all ADV students are alike in their readiness levels, interests, and learning styles. A student should only compact out of regular class activities when lessons review reading and writing concepts and skills with which the student has already demonstrated proficiency. Has a student already acted a major role in or read *Romeo and Juliet* in its entirety and works well quickly and independently, but needs work in close reading skills and literary analysis? That student's independent learning contract may require that she complete several close reading activities independently and write an in-depth essay on the play with accelerated standards. Has a student demonstrated the ability to read more quickly and comprehend more deeply Shakespeare's language? That student may need an accelerated reading schedule and opportunities to work with other ADV students on ADV CR assignments. Has a student demonstrated the ability to write in-depth literary analysis but never read much if any Shakespeare? That student may be able to skip whole-class instruction on essay writing and instead work independently on an ADV essay topic.

d. Projects for compacting students should be challenging acceleration opportunities (chances to practice higher-level content and skills) or enrichment opportunities (chances to explore more deeply a subject or an interest). Be careful not to substitute quantity for quality in designing compacting projects. Just because a student learns quickly does not mean she or he should not take the time to plumb the depths of one subject. For project ideas, see the Compacting Fun handout (pages 88–91). You might also ask students to design their rubrics after conferencing with you.

e. Allow compacting students to participate in meaningful WCAs. Have compacting students participate in such WCAs as dramatic performance, Socratic discussion, and cinematic analysis. In these settings, a compacting student who may be a strong reader will get to see other peers take the lead in roles such as directing, visual-spatial analysis, and interpersonal communication and leadership. Many gifted students have multiple talents and should not be isolated from the rich variety of learning opportunities afforded by WCAs. Compacting students should rarely disappear for the entire unit unless the student needs grade acceleration.

f. For all independent compacting work, provide a learning contract that the student signs, a work schedule with a task log so that you can check it daily or weekly, and rubrics for products and performances. You will have to schedule at least one face-to-face conference each week if a student is missing a significant amount of class. Seek the support of media specialists or parent and other community mentors so other adults can check in with compacting students and provide the individualized attention needed.

g. Arrange at least a once-weekly conference with compacting students to monitor progress; provide written or audio feedback on any submissions of work.

h. Provide opportunities for compacting students to present projects to the class.

Handout PRO.d.1: Very Punny

A pun is a noun meaning "a play on words." There are several ways to pun (also a verb). Think of it as a sport like a spelling bee or the game Scrabble in which you demonstrate your word knowledge.

1. You can use the word multiple times for all its different senses or meanings. (Demonstrate your knowledge of **denotation** and **connotation**.)

2. You can use two similar-sounding words or two words that have similar meanings. (Demonstrate your knowledge of denotation and rhyme.)

3. You can use several words that relate by theme while using a word with multiple meanings. (Demonstrate your knowledge of connotation and theme.) An example: "The wife was so *glad* that her husband was finally taking out the *trash* that she didn't *trash* him for once."

4. You can change a letter or two to create a new word that is a blend of these meanings. For example, *funny + pun = punny*. (Demonstrate your creativity and sense of humor.)

Directions:
You will rewrite the first exchange of the play *Romeo and Juliet* into modern language. In this scene, two Capulet servants, strutting through the streets of Verona, boast about what they will do should they run into any of "the house of Montague."

1. Read the Shakespeare text in the Scene for Very Punny section once through. Then return to brainstorm today's slang expressions and any other expressions as prompted so that you can translate the scene into modern language.

2. Create a brief skit of the same number of lines and same content using today's puns. Translate the modernized Shakespeare into something "very punny." Get it?☺ And that's *punny*, not hilariously *funny*, so don't worry so much about whether your classmates will laugh as much as try to create the four types of puns described above using today's language.

3. Check with me if you think a pun using a curse word or a sexual **innuendo** might work. I must approve it first. Shakespeare was an adult writing for adults, whereas our

classroom and its student authors work in a very different **context**.

4. Once you've created your skit, practice it as well as an explanation of Shakespeare's puns to present to the class.

Glossary:
connotation: associations, suggestions, and implications of a word beyond its dictionary definition
context: situation, environment
denotation: literal or dictionary definition
innuendo: a suggestion or hint

Scene for Very Punny

Enter Sampson and Gregory, with swords and bucklers, of the house of Capulet.

SAMPSON: Gregory, on my word, we'll not *carry coals*.

Translation: receive insults or suffer insults. This was a slang expression of the time, to bear indignities without a fight, perhaps because the occupation of selling and carrying coal left one quite dirty. Coal carrying was considered a low occupation.
Brainstorm: What expressions do we have today for "suffering insults" or "being insulted"?

GREGORY: No, for then we should be *colliers*.

Translation: coal dealers—known as a low, dirty, and dishonest trade.
Brainstorm: What occupations today are looked on as "low"? Note: Whatever profession you end up mocking, if there's even a one percent chance that someone's family member in our class is involved in it, be sure to make a **disclaimer** first that no personal offense is intended and that the characters of Samson and Gregory are not intelligent nor admirable guys. Their speech is rough, rude, and mocking.

SAMPSON: I mean, *and we be in choler*, we'll *draw*.

Translation: (a) *and we be in choler* means "if we are angry." Sampson is punning on *collier* and *choler*, which were similar-sounding words in Shakespeare's day; (b) *draw* means "pull out one's sword."
Brainstorm: What expressions do we have today for *angry* that might work with the words you've used earlier for being angry and low pro-

fessions? And what is a modern expression for pulling out a weapon or starting a fight?

GREGORY: Ay, while you live, *draw your neck out of collar*.

Translation: *draw your neck out of collar* means "stay as far away as possible from the hangman's noose," which was a popular form of execution back then.
Brainstorm: What forms of execution, punishment, or danger might be puns with the words you've used for being angry and low professions?

SAMPSON: I strike quickly, being *moved*.

Translation: *moved* means "motivated" or "aroused" or "inspired."
Brainstorm: What expressions do we have for *inspire, arouse, catalyze toward a fight*? Note: Shakespeare uses a play on the word *move* later in this scene where it means "sexual arousal."

GREGORY: But thou art not quickly *moved* to strike.

Translation: Gregory is teasing that though Sampson might think he strikes quickly, he's not easily inspired to fight—which implies that he's a coward.
Brainstorm: Can you play on words the way Gregory has played on *quickly*? Note how he's switched the word arrangement to mock Sampson.

Glossary:
disclaimer: a denial of any intent to offend

Teaching Romeo and Juliet: *A Differentiated Approach* by Delia DeCourcy, Lyn Fairchild, and Robin Follet © 2007 NCTE.

Handout PRO.d.2: So You'd Like to Compact Shakespeare

If you have this handout, you meet at least two of the following criteria for *Romeo and Juliet*:

1. You've already read and understood an **unabridged** original-language version.

2. You've performed and understood several unabridged, original-language scenes.

3. You've seen the play in a live theater, watched more than one film version, and/or have read several original-language scenes from the play, and you understood them.

4. You've already read and understood the entirety of an unabridged, original-language version of another Shakespeare play.

5. You understand more than 80 percent of the Shakespeare passages we have been translating, and you feel you can read the play independently without much coaching. Along with your skill of quick and accurate comprehension, you would prefer to work more in depth and at a greater level of challenge than you imagine daily lessons in class will provide.

What Is Compacting?

Compacting is a specialized learning program for advanced students who have demonstrated through **preassessments** the knowledge of grade-level content and skill **proficiency**. If you "compact out" (are excused) from certain standard grade-level activities for *Romeo and Juliet*, you will work on **enrichment** or **accelerated** studies instead. You may return to whole-class activities at various times as directed.

Yes, I Meet at Least Two of the Criteria Above: What's Next?

You will need to pass quizzes on acts 1, 2, 3, 4, and 5 of *Romeo and Juliet*. To do so, you have one of two options:

1. For those who've already read most or all of the play, review the play. I will give you a deadline by which you have to take the assessments, all in one period. You will need to pass 80 percent of all the questions, including any oral quizzes I give. Take the time to skim the play

and review the action. Make an outline of notes. Do not use study aids such as online or print notes, but spend time in the actual text. You will be doing close reading exercises of Shakespeare's text later, and it is essential that you are familiar with the text.

2. For those who believe you can read the play on your own without much assistance, read the first few pages of the play on your own and then bring me your suggested timeline for completing the play. Create a reasonable reading schedule that lets me know how many pages you can read per night.

IMPORTANT REMINDERS:

1. Do not share your knowledge of these assessments with other students who have not yet taken them.

2. Compacting is not a permanent learning modification. It is based on this unit. If you do not meet the expectations we agree on for your specialized learning program, we will revisit our arrangement and make whatever changes are necessary.

Assuming I Pass the Assessments, What Happens Next?

When you conference with me, you will receive an activity and project list for enrichment and accelerated studies, and then establish a work schedule and timeline of daily activities. You will spend class time on these activities in the classroom or another work space. Occasionally you will rejoin the class. Please note: if you have other suggestions about schedules and project ideas, please bring them to my attention.

Glossary:
accelerated: advanced, above grade-level expectations
enrichment: advanced in terms of depth and interest level, but not necessarily accelerated to above grade level
preassessment: a pretest or quiz taken before a unit begins to show your prior level of knowledge and skill
proficiency: at-standard performance; the state of meeting grade-level expectations
unabridged: complete, not shortened

Act 1, Scene 1

Lesson 1.a: Vexed in Verona

Student Content and Skill Understandings

- Prepare to read and engage with a Shakespeare text: summarize, define, predict, translate, highlight. (AS)
- Identify and explicate orally and in writing a character's traits using the character's actions, speech, appearance, and reactions from other characters. (AS)
- Identify and explicate orally the reasoning behind an argument. (AS)

Themes

- Rebellion
- Lust
- Dichotomy and paradox

Materials and Handouts

- 1.a.1: Pre-Play Poll handout
- OPTIONAL. Mini-Lesson 2: Would You Believe What They Did Back Then? (see page 152)
- 1.a.2: Vexed in Verona handout
- OPTIONAL. 1.b.1: Shakescholar Close Reader, Scene 1, A, B, and C (see pages 53–60)
- PRO.a.3 and PRO.c.1: Act 1 Journals and Tips for Tackling the Language (see pages 17 and 25)
- Dictionaries and Shakespeare glossary
- OPTIONAL. Props such as swords and bucklers for performing act 1, scene 1: plastic swords, yardsticks, and paper plates decorated with insignias of *C* or *M*
- Franco Zeffirelli's and Baz Luhrmann's film versions of *Romeo and Juliet*

Activities

STEP 1. WCA: Pre-Play Poll (20 minutes)

1. Explain to students that many debatable issues and themes will arise during the study of *Romeo and Juliet* and that they may find themselves changing their opinions because of what they observe in the play or, by the end, holding more steadfastly to their original opinions.

2. Ask students to complete the Pre-Play Poll, which asks them to take an initial stand on an issue or theme, in a kinesthetic or written exercise. Options include:

   a. The Human Graph: Read aloud each statement and ask students to move to an AGREE, DIS-AGREE, or UNDECIDED side of the room each time. After students have responded to each statement, ask one student from each position to explain his or her choice. Those UNDECIDED can also share any questions they have. This approach asks for their gut reactions, followed by discussion. Encourage students to define words from the poll such as *offensive* or *supportive* using their own examples. They should debate words such as *desperate* to determine what would be a "desperate" response to a "desperate" situation. After such discussions, ask if anyone wants to change positions.

   b. Paper Poll: Distribute the poll as a handout and have the students circle their responses independently. Ask students to move into pairs or triads to discuss answers, and as with the Human Graph, encourage students to define terms used in the poll with their own examples to see if they can come to small-group consensus; then come back together as a whole class. Determine whether there was a majority response for each question and if so, why?

STEP 2. OPTIONAL. WCA: Mini-Lesson 2: Would You Believe What They Did Back Then? (20 minutes)

This mini-lesson (see page 152) establishes the Elizabethan social relationships in this scene.

STEP 3. Read-Through Scene 1 (30 minutes)

1. Explain how scene 1 is the play's exposition and the purpose of exposition. Ask students to predict, based on the Prologue, what Shakespeare might reveal here to his audience.

2. Explain that the class is going to explore part of act 1, scene 1 as actors and directors. Everyone will simulate actors trying out for *Romeo and Juliet*. Needed: streetwise guys looking for a fight because they are loyal to two different families.

3. Ask ADV students to read from line 1 of the scene in their playscripts through "Nay, as they dare" to help explain puns, and reinforce, or have them reinforce, the importance of using Tips for Tackling the Language strategies. You might explain the sexual punning in greater detail depending on your students, your school community, and your comfort level. Slapstick usage of swords to imply erections and other sexual references have been the standbys for Shakespeare actors in the past. As students giggle, you might ask, Why is lust funny to us? Humor comes from not only elements of surprise but also violating the taboo—broaching the inappropriate (i.e., the private brought into the public). We also laugh at the exaggeration of character and the folly of human behavior, as in Sampson's inflated ego and need to brag about his sexual prowess, which is quickly mocked by Gregory's scorn and doubt.

4. Arrange all students to stand in a circle and give them the Vexed in Verona handout, which picks up the playscript from where students stopped reading. Instruct students to read through the handout once slowly, one by one around the circle, so that all read aloud at least one line and repeating as necessary. Then have one round where students read as fast as they can through the scene, each person taking just one word.

5. Ask for word definitions. Model skills 1–7 from the Tips for Tackling the Language handout to help stu-

dents understand words like *washing*.

6. Ask for volunteers to stand and read in a variety of voices and paces to show "rebelliousness."

7. Ask volunteers to perform with props. Ask the class to compliment and direct.

8. Ask TR questions. Call on students who can answer or stretch to answer these questions:

    a. NOV:

        i. What are we supposed to think of the behavior of these servants?

        ii. What specific actions demonstrate this behavior?

        iii. Why are these two groups of men fighting?

    b. OT:

        i. What information do these men use to make their decision to fight?

        ii. Do you think they have any other motivations to fight? How do you know? What specific words demonstrate those motivations?

    c. OT/ADV: How do the themes of rebellion, dichotomy, and paradox appear within the action and characterization?

9. Watch the Zeffirelli and Luhrmann versions of this scene and ask students to comment on representations of the theme of rebelliousness in the characters. In what ways do the actors show rebellion? What is the filmmaker saying about rebellion? (You can discuss whether he glorifies or critiques or even condemns rebellion. If your class is mostly NOV, give them these three options to discuss.) Ask students to select their favorite Sampson and Gregory and justify their choice.

Epilogue: Suggested Homework

We recommend that you assign creative writing skill strand assignments (see page 137) rather than assigning independent reading to the majority of the class. Compacting students should be reading right now in preparation for preassessments and developing tentative reading and task schedules as needed for you to approve. If your department or school standards demand that you keep to a certain teaching timeline, assign Shakespeare CR activities 1.b.1 A, B, and C (see pages 53–60), which ask students to read closely and interpret the action that follows the fight. See page 51, Notes on Differentiation, to learn the differences among the handouts.

Notes on Differentiation

1. The Pre-Play Poll allows all students to express opinions and engage with themes while engaging in higher-order critical thinking skills as a learning community.

2. The slow- and fast-paced read-arounds of handout 1.a.2: Vexed in Verona allow students to savor and play with language without feeling the pressure of comprehending every word. For more dramatic exercises that allow students to gain comfort with the text, we recommend that you use the Folger Library's Shakespeare Set Free series (O'Brien).

3. All students, including ADV, need the reinforcement of the reading strategies taught by the Tips for Tackling the Language handout. If slow, impatient, and/or quick learners chafe at the close reading approach, ask them to practice patience and trust the process. Mortimer Adler's advocacy of slow and thorough reading is a good reminder to them, as is pulling students for a private, two-line translation demonstration at the beginning or end of class. If an impatient student cannot quickly paraphrase Shakespeare's meaning back to you, she or he may see the point of slowing the reading down.

4. Creative writing skill strand assignments allow students to further engage with themes of the play by means of personal connections, which promote greater investment, ownership, and retention of the play's characters, plot, and themes.

Handout 1.a.1: Pre-Play Poll

Directions: Decide whether you AGREE, DISAGREE, or are UNDE-CIDED about the following statements. There is no right answer for any

1. It is all right to engage someone in a fight if they make **offensive** statements.

    AGREE   DISAGREE   UNDECIDED

2. It is all right to keep important problems in your life se-cret from your parents if they will get angry and punish you.

    AGREE   DISAGREE   UNDECIDED

3. Parents should not have a role in determining whom their children marry.

    AGREE   DISAGREE   UNDECIDED

4. **Deceiving** people **temporarily** is all right if it is for a good cause in the long run.

    AGREE   DISAGREE   UNDECIDED

5. Always be supportive of friends and family even if you disagree with their choices.

    AGREE   DISAGREE   UNDECIDED

6. If you fall in love with someone of whom your family disapproves, you should marry the person regardless of the **obstacles**.

    AGREE   DISAGREE   UNDECIDED

7. Parents are **ultimately** responsible for their children's choices.

    AGREE   DISAGREE   UNDECIDED

8. Love at first sight does exist.

    AGREE   DISAGREE   UNDECIDED

9. **Desperate** situations call for desperate measures

　　　AGREE　　　DISAGREE　　　UNDECIDED

10. It's all right to **resort to** violence when the honor of friends or family is at stake.

　　　AGREE　　　DISAGREE　　　UNDECIDED

Glossary:
deceiving: lying
desperate: dangerous or risky
obstacles: problems or things that stand in the way
offensive: rude, cruel, hurtful
resort to: choose
temporarily: for now, for a short period
ultimately: in the end

Teaching Romeo and Juliet: *A Differentiated Approach* by Delia DeCourcy, Lyn Fairchild, and Robin Follet © 2007 NCTE.

Handout 1.a.2: Vexed in Verona

Shakespeare Text	My Notes

SAMPSON: . . . I will bite my thumb at them,
which is disgrace to them if they bear it.

ABRAM: Do you bite your thumb at us, sir?

SAMPSON: I do bite my thumb, sir.

ABRAM: Do you bite your thumb at us, sir?

SAMPSON: [*Aside* to Gregory] Is the law of our side if I say ay?

GREGORY: [*Aside* to Sampson] No.

SAMPSON: No, sir, I do not bite my thumb at you, sir,
but I bite my thumb, sir.

GREGORY: Do you quarrel, sir?

ABRAM: Quarrel, sir? No, sir.

SAMPSON: But if you do, sir, I am for you. I serve
as good a man as you.

ABRAM: No better.

SAMPSON: Well, sir.

Enter Benvolio

GREGORY: [*Aside* to Sampson] Say "better," here comes one
of my master's kinsmen.

SAMPSON: Yes, better, sir.

ABRAM: You lie.

SAMPSON: Draw, if you be men. Gregory, remember thy washing blow.

Teaching Romeo and Juliet: *A Differentiated Approach* by Delia DeCourcy, Lyn Fairchild, and Robin Follet © 2007 NCTE.

Lesson 1.b: Vexed in Verona

Student Content and Skill Understandings

- Prepare to read and engage with a Shakespeare text: summarize, define, predict, translate, highlight. (AS)

- Summarize plot, identify narrative structure, and explain cause and effect relationships orally and in writing; predict plot outcomes based on narrative structure. (AS)

- Identify and explicate orally and in writing a character's traits using the character's actions, speech, appearance, and reactions from other characters. (OT/ADV)

- Use literary terms to articulate interpretations of characters, narrative, and themes: *metaphor, simile, oxymoron* (AS); *blank verse, iambic pentameter* (ADV).

Themes

- Rebellion
- Dichotomy and paradox

Materials and Handouts

- 1.b.1: Shakescholar Close Reader, Scene 1, A, B, and C
- 1.b.2: Shakescholar Close Reader, Scene 1, A, B, and C
- PRO.c.1: Tips for Tackling the Language handout (see page 25)
- Dictionaries and Shakespeare glossary
- Franco Zeffirelli's and Baz Luhrmann's film versions of *Romeo and Juliet*

Activities

STEP 1. WCA: Review of Themes (10 minutes)

Ask students to write on a theme question as an anchoring activity, or ask for student feedback on themes using their journal entries, discussions of statements from the Pre-Play Poll handout, or Socratic discussion questions (see page 145).

STEP 2. TR Groups: Shakescholar Close Reader 1.b.1: Scene 1, A, B, and C (35 minutes)

1. Divide students by readiness to translate lines using CRs that start from Benvolio's line, "Part, fools!" and end with the Prince's line, "Once more, on pain of death . . ." Distribute Shakescholar Close Reader 1.b.1 A, B, and C to appropriate groups (NOV, OT, and ADV, respectively). Note that the handouts provide places for you to insert line numbers since your text edition may be numbered differently. Explain the activity (see Notes on Differentiation on page 51 for this lesson to learn the differences among handouts) and review roles and expectations. Tell students that they must use the BARD It! strategy. Circulate while students work, and provide assistance. Remember that you can assign sections of these CRs and not cover every word of the scene.

2. As students submit close readers to you, ask them to indicate their favorite part of the handout. What best assisted their comprehension of the scene?

3. Have the Symbolist for 1.b.1 CRs A and B submit pictures to you; use the best submissions as review for next day's class. Show these illustrations to the class and ask for artists to review what incidents occurred in the text read the previous day.

STEP 3. WCA: Review of Themes (5 minutes)

Ask students to share answers to questions on their CRs that relate to the themes of rebellion and dichotomy and paradox.

Epilogue: Suggested Homework

1. Assign Shakescholar Close Reader 1.b.2: Scene 1, A, B, and C. Provide supplementary reading materials for NOV and OT students (see Chapter 1, page 7).

   a. NOV students complete plot summary and apply definitions so that you can assess their basic knowledge and comprehension of narrative events as well as figurative language such as *oxymoron* and *metaphor*.

   b. OT students complete plot summary and apply definitions so that you can assess their basic knowledge and comprehension of narrative events as well as figurative language such as *oxymoron* and *metaphor*.

   c. ADV students evaluate Romeo by the standards of a Petrarchan lover; students also identify and evaluate oxymorons and metaphors, allowing you to assess comprehension and application of material.

2. Compacting students should be reading or reviewing the play and preparing for assessments. Close Reader C handouts are always appropriate future close reading assignments.

Notes on Differentiation

1. These skills are assessed in Shakescholar Close Reader 1.b.1 A, B, and C and Close Reader 1.b.2 A, B, and C:

   a. NOV students use symbols to complete a plot summary, questions, and predictions so that you can assess their basic knowledge and comprehension of narrative events.

   b. OT students use phrases and sentences to summarize the plot and analyze character relationships by analyzing prose, blank verse, and puns so that you can assess their basic knowledge and comprehension as well as their analytical skills.

   c. ADV students read and analyze the Prince's speech in depth while predicting plot outcomes so that you can assess their basic knowledge and comprehension of narrative events and characters as well as analytical skills of cause and effect.

2. When you assess student work on CRs, pay close attention to which students stretch themselves with the challenge questions. If a student later seems ready to move up a level with a close reader, provide him or her with that opportunity.

3. If students struggle with circling key words on these CRs, consider teaching a mini-lesson on "finding the key word." You can stress that nouns, verbs, and adjectives often contain key themes and to look for these. Remind students of the main themes you are exploring and to

keep an eye out for any synonyms or words that carry weight and significance through their connotations. Try a free association exercise in which you ask students to think of as many synonyms as they can for the word *old* and then discuss how writing "the elderly lady" is different from writing "the old lady" or "the prehistoric lady" or "the crusty lady," which have greatly different connotations. Students need to pay close attention on a word-by-word level to get Shakespeare's power.

Shakescholar Close Reader 1.b.1: Scene 1, A

Act 1, Scene 1, Lines _____ – _____

From Benvolio's line, "Part, fools!" to Lady Montague's line, "Thou shalt not stir one foot to seek a foe."

Facilitator: Reads directions and keeps the group on task.

Readers: Read the text aloud in small chunks, stopping when the Explicator asks.

Explicator: Guides group in translating the lines into modern language, stopping the Reader every few lines. Everyone should assist the Explicator in the translation process.

Researcher: Uses the book references, a dictionary, or a glossary to define unknown words.

Symbolist: Designs an easy-to-draw **literal** picture or **symbol** that will help everyone remember plot events.

You will need your Tips for Tackling the Language handout.

To Read:

1. Choose group roles and open your books to act 1, scene 1, and the first line indicated at the top of this page.

2. Have the Reader read the first few lines of text. Stop where you think the complete thought ends.

3. Have the Explicator translate and the Researcher provide references. Be sure to use your Tips for Tackling the Language handout.

4. Have the Facilitator lead a discussion to propose a symbol for the first six lines.

5. Have the Symbolist draw it and everyone copy it on their close reader.

6. Proceed through the rest of the text in this manner, ending at the following words: "Thou shalt not stir one foot to seek a foe."

Glossary:
literal: realistic (if the text mentions an apple, and an apple is important to the action, draw an apple)
symbol: a drawing that represents an idea (if the text mentions love, draw a heart)

Plot Summary:
Sampson, Gregory, Abram, and Balthasar are fighting. Benvolio (Romeo's friend) tries to stop them; Tybalt (Juliet's cousin) fights Benvolio. Police officers and citizens of Verona appear to stop the fighting. Lord Capulet and Lord Montague threaten each other.

To Discuss:

1. Why doesn't Tybalt accept Benvolio's statement that he is trying to keep the peace?

   _____

2. Why do you think so many people of Verona would get involved in a servants' fight?

   _____

3. What are Lady Capulet and Lady Montague trying to do?

   _____

4. Why does Lady Capulet say Lord Capulet should call for a "crutch"?

   _____

5. Think of any experience you might have witnessed or been involved in in which something small (such as an insult) ended up creating something big (such as a **brawl**). What do you think Shakespeare might be pointing out to the audience about the city of Verona?

   _____

6. **CHALLENGE QUESTION:** What might Shakespeare be showing about human nature in this scene?

   _____

Glossary:
brawl: quarrel or noisy fight

In the space below, predict three possible outcomes that could happen in the story, based on this scene. Indicate the incident that would cause the outcome.

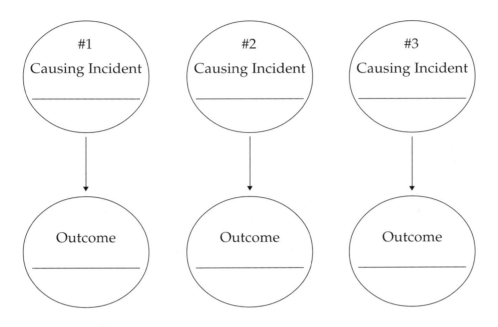

Shakescholar Close Reader 1.b.1: Scene 1, B

Act 1, Scene 1, Lines _____–_____

From Benvolio's line, "Part, fools!" to Lady Montague's line, "Thou shalt not stir one foot to seek a foe."

> *Facilitator*: Reads directions and keeps the group on task.
>
> *Readers*: Read the text aloud in small chunks, stopping when the Explicator asks.
>
> *Explicator*: Guides the group in translating the lines into modern language, stopping the Reader every few lines. Everyone should assist the Explicator in the translation process.
>
> *Researcher*: Uses the book references, a dictionary, or a glossary to define unknown words.
>
> *Summarizer*: Suggests key words, phrases, or a sentence that will help everyone remember the events of the plot up to a certain line and asks everyone in the group for input.

You will need your Tips for Tackling the Language handout.

To Read:

1. Choose group roles and open your books to act 1, scene 1, and the first line indicated above.

2. Have the Reader read the first six lines of text.

3. Have the Explicator translate and the Researcher provide references. Be sure to use your Tips for Tackling the Language handout.

4. Have the Summarizer lead a discussion after identifying possible key words, phrases, or a sentence that will help everyone remember the events of the plot up to a certain line.

5. Proceed through the rest of the text in this manner, ending at "Thou shalt not stir one foot to seek a foe."

Plot Summary:

Sampson, Gregory, Abram, and Balthasar are fighting. Benvolio (Romeo's friend) tries to stop them; Tybalt (Juliet's cousin) mocks Benvolio. Police officers and citizens of Verona try to stop the fighting. Lord and Lady Capulet and Lord and Lady Montague appear; the Lords threaten one another; the Ladies plead with their husbands to get them to stop.

To Discuss:

1. What pun does Tybalt use in the line that begins "What, art thou drawn . . ."? How do its meanings indicate his character?

2. There are two types of fighters in this scene. What are these types and which characters fall into these categories? (Hint: Tybalt speaks of this **dichotomy** when he enters the scene.)

3. Note that servants are speaking in prose—everyday speech—while Benvolio, Tybalt, the Lords, and the Ladies speak in blank verse (approximately ten syllables per line, every second syllable stressed; also known as iambic pentameter). Why would Shakespeare distinguish their speech?

4. If the citizens of Verona appear quickly on the scene armed and ready to stop the fight, what does that tell you about the history before the play begins? How does this **exposition foreshadow** the rest of the play? In the space below, predict three possible outcomes that could occur, based on this scene.

Glossary:
dichotomy: a division into two opposing groups
exposition: the beginning of the play in which the characters, conflict, and setting are introduced
foreshadow: predict

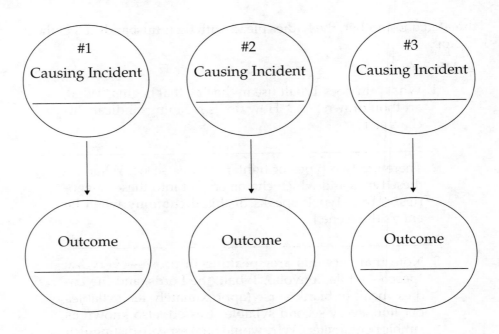

Shakescholar Close Reader 1.b.1: Scene 1, C

Act 1, Scene 1, Lines _____–_____

To Read:

1. Choose a Facilitator to read these directions and keep the group on task. You will be reading from the Prince's entrance through his entire speech.

2. Assign a Narrator to read the stage directions and any references.

3. Assign an Explicator, the person who stops the reading every six to ten lines to lead the discussion for translating them into modern language. Use your Tips for Tackling the Language handout. Everyone should assist the Explicator.

To Discuss:

1. Read the Prince's speech a second time. Then agree as a group on answers to the following:

    a. What important historical information does the Prince convey?

    b. What are two important political decisions the Prince makes?

2. Evaluate the Prince's political decisions. How sound are they? Determine your criteria for a sound political decision. What do these decisions establish for the rest of the drama?

3. Note that servants were speaking in **prose** while Benvolio, Tybalt, the Lords, the Ladies, and the Prince speak in **blank verse**. What conclusions can you draw about why Shakespeare would distinguish their speech?

4. Agree on the most important lines within his speech and be ready to explain why.

5. Analyze the following circled words.

    a. Define each word by using the dictionary, glossary, and text references to learn the word meanings. In what context do they appear in act 1, scene 1? Write a definition for each inside the appropriate circle.

      b. What are the various **connotations** of these words? Brainstorm at least four connotations of each word and write these around each word using the lines provided.

      c. How might these words connect to the themes we are studying in this play? Connect these words to themes by drawing arrows. Be prepared to explain the connections.

Glossary:

blank verse: approximately ten syllables per line, every second syllable stressed; also known as iambic pentameter.

connotation: associations, suggestions, and implications of a word beyond its dictionary definition

prose: everyday speech

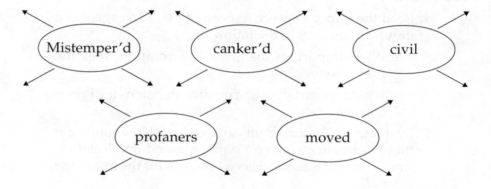

Themes:

Love & Marriage   Rebellion   Fate   Dichotomy & Paradox   Identity

Connections We See:

Teaching Romeo and Juliet: *A Differentiated Approach* by Delia DeCourcy, Lyn Fairchild, and Robin Follet © 2007 NCTE.

Shakescholar Close Reader 1.b.2: Scene 1, A

Act 1, Scene 1, Selected Lines

Understanding the Scene

YOUR TASK: Answer the questions after each passage from *Romeo and Juliet*. Complete the Challenge Questions if you dare!

Scene Summary:

Romeo's parents (Lord and Lady Montague) are worried about their son and ask Romeo's good friend and cousin, Benvolio, how Romeo is doing. The three of them speak in the town square after the big fight between the Montagues and the Capulets. Romeo was not involved in the fight. In the excerpt below, Lord Montague describes Romeo's mysterious behavior.

Directions:

- Read the lines that Lord Montague, Romeo's father, speaks to Benvolio, Romeo's cousin and friend.
- Use your Tips for Tackling the Language handout to decode the meaning.
- Circle the key word or phrase in each line.

MONTAGUE: Away from light steals home my heavy son,

And private in his chamber pens himself,

Shuts up his windows, locks fair daylight out,

And makes himself an artificial night:

Black and portentous must his humor prove,

Unless good counsel may the cause remove.
(lines ___–___)

1. What is Romeo doing that causes his parents to worry?

_____

2. What kind of mood has Romeo been in lately?

_____

3. Which words or lines support your description of Romeo's mood?

_____

4. When you are in a similar mood, what do you usually do?

_____

The Heart of the Problem: Romeo to Benvolio

In this scene, Romeo uses a form of figurative language, an oxymoron, which is opposites paired in a phrase or description. You see and hear oxymorons all the time: on TV commercials, on restaurant menus, and in political talk.

Examples:

- Bittersweet: How can something be both bitter and sweet? But some chocolate is!

- Jumbo shrimp: How can a small thing be big, since *shrimp* means "small"? But go to certain restaurants and you'll find this dish on the menu!

Explain these opposites with a question and an explanation, following the models above:

peace force

- _____ ?

- _____ !

firm pillow

- _____ ?

- _____ !

alone in a crowd

- _____ ?

- _____ !

CHALLENGE QUESTION: Write oxymorons you find in everyday life below.

_____

If you research oxymorons in another print or electronic source, give credit to the source below (list the title of the book, radio show, TV show, film, or the Web URL):

_____

Romeo uses oxymorons to describe to Benvolio why he is feeling so depressed. He is in love with Rosaline, a beautiful woman who does not return his feelings. She says she has sworn to live **chaste**. Because she is not interested, he feels **unrequited love** for Rosaline.

Glossary:
chaste: virginal (the state of remaining a virgin)
unrequited love: love that is not returned

CHALLENGE QUESTION (OPTIONAL): Have you ever felt unrequited love or known anyone who has? List the adjectives to describe the way the lover feels when his or her love is unrequited.

- Read Romeo's speech to Benvolio below in which he describes his unrequited love for Rosaline. Use your Tips for Tackling the Language handout to translate.
- Circle all the oxymorons you see.

ROMEO: Here's much to do with hate, but more with love:

Why then, O brawling love, O loving hate,

O anything of nothing first create!

O heavy lightness, serious vanity,

Misshapen chaos of well-seeming forms,

Feather of lead, bright smoke, cold fire, sick health,

Still-waking sleep, that is not what it is!

This love feel I, that feel no love in this.
(lines ___–___)

1. How many oxymorons did you find? _____

2. **CHALLENGE QUESTION:** Why would Romeo use oxymorons to describe his feelings about unrequited love?

_____

3. **CHALLENGE QUESTION:** Is love ever the way Romeo says it is? Why or why not?

_____

Let's learn about another type of figurative language that Romeo uses in this scene.

Metaphor: a comparison between two unlike things in which one thing is substituted for another. A metaphor is like a math equation, where A = B. For example, we might say to someone, "You're a pig!" Obviously, the person is not actually a pig, but there is one way that the human and the pig can be alike: they both share the qualities of greediness or sloppiness.

Directions:

1. Read Romeo's description of love below. Use the Tips for Tackling the Language handout.

2. Romeo is just full of metaphors today. List the six things that love is equated with; find the six different sides of the equation.

ROMEO: Love is a smoke made with the fume of sighs,

Being purg'd, a fire sparkling in lover's eyes,

Being vex'd, a sea nourish'd with loving tears.

What is it else? a madness most discreet,

A choking gall, and a preserving sweet.
(lines ___–___)

a. Love = _____

b. Love = _____

c. Love = _____

d. Love = _____

e. Love = _____

f. Love = _____

3. What metaphor do you believe best describes love? Why?

CHALLENGE QUESTION: To what unlike person, place, or thing would you compare love? Why? Write two metaphors. Example: Love is an ocean: warm on the sunny days and cold on the stormy days.

Teaching Romeo and Juliet: *A Differentiated Approach* by Delia DeCourcy, Lyn Fairchild, and Robin Follet © 2007 NCTE.

Shakescholar Close Reader 1.b.2: Scene 1, B

Act 1, Scene 1, Lines _____ – _____

From Lord Montague's line, "Who set this ancient quarrel . . .?" to Benvolio's line, "I'll pay that doctrine."

Understanding the Scene
Directions:

- Use your copy of the play to read specified lines from act 1, scene 1.

- As you read, use your Tips for Tackling the Language handout.

- Scene Summary: In this scene that occurs right after the fight between the Montagues and the Capulets in Verona's town square, Romeo's parents express their concern about Romeo to Romeo's good friend and cousin, Benvolio. Benvolio speaks to Romeo to determine the reasons for his **melancholy**, Romeo admits he's having romance problems, and then Benvolio gives advice to Romeo about his **dilemma**.

Glossary:
dilemma: problem
melancholy: depression

What the Parents and Best Friend Think

1. Read from Lord Montague's line, "Who set this ancient quarrel . . .?" to "Come madam, let's away." Use the Tips for Tackling the Language handout.

2. Identify key word or phrases as you read in order to answer these questions:

   a. What is Romeo doing that causes his parents to worry? _____

   _____

   b. What kind of mood has Romeo been in lately?

   _____

   _____

The Heart of the Problem: Romeo to Benvolio
Romeo uses oxymorons to describe to Benvolio his feelings of **unrequited love** for a woman named Rosaline, a beauty who does not return his feelings because she says she has sworn to live chaste.

Oxymoron: the use of opposites paired in a phrase or description. An oxymoron is a situation, place, or thing where opposites co-exist. You see and hear oxymorons all the time: on TV commercials, on restaurant menus, and in political talk. Examples: *jumbo shrimp, bittersweet, peace force, firm pillow, alone in a crowd.*

Below, create your own oxymoron or record ones that you are familiar with:

If you research oxymorons in another print or electronic source, give credit to the source below (list the title of the book, radio show, TV show, film, or the Web URL):

Glossary:
unrequited love: love that is not returned

Poor Lovelorn Romeo . . .

1. Read from Benvolio's line, "Good morrow, cousin," to Romeo's line, "Dost thou not laugh?" to learn more about Romeo's woes. Use your Tips for Tackling the Language handout. Identify key words or phrases that answer this question: Why is Romeo sad?

2. Reread Romeo's speech to Benvolio below. Highlight or circle key words.

3. Circle all the oxymorons you see.

ROMEO: Here's much to do with hate, but more with love:

Why then, O brawling love, O loving hate,

O anything of nothing first create!

O heavy lightness, serious vanity,

Misshapen chaos of well-seeming forms,

Feather of lead, bright smoke, cold fire, sick
    health,

Still-waking sleep, that is not what it is!

This love feel I, that feel no love in this.
(lines ___–___)

1. How does Romeo feel about love? How do you know?
   (Hint: If he uses oxymorons, how does this indicate how
   he is feeling? Quote a few oxymorons in your answer.)

   _____

   _____

2. Have you felt this way about love before? Why or why
   not? _____

   _____

Metaphor: a comparison between two unlike things in which one thing
is substituted for another. A metaphor is like a math equation, where A
= B. For example, we might say to someone, "You're a pig!" Obviously,
the person is not actually a pig, but there is one way that the human
and the pig can be alike: they both share the qualities of greediness or
sloppiness. A metaphor carries more power than a simile because the
comparison is stated without calling attention to itself with words such
as *like* or *as*, as in a simile.

1. Read Romeo's description of love below. Use the Tips
   for Tackling the Language handout.

2. Circle the metaphors.

3. Create six metaphorical equations from this description
   Romeo gives us. Fill out both sides of the metaphor equation below (hint: one side of the equation stays the same)
   and write them in order of your favorite to least favorite.

ROMEO: Love is a smoke made with the fume of sighs,

      Being purg'd, a fire sparkling in lover's eyes,

      Being vex'd, a sea nourish'd with loving tears.

      What is it else? a madness most discreet,

      A choking gall, and a preserving sweet.
      (lines ___–___)

    a. _____ = _____

    b. _____ = _____

    c. _____ = _____

    d. _____ = _____

    e. _____ = _____

    f. _____ = _____

1. Why does Romeo compare love to the following? List the **connotations** when this kind of a comparison appears.

Glossary:

connotations: associations, suggestions, and implications of a word beyond its dictionary definition

METAPHOR	CONNOTATIONS
Love is a smoke	
Love is a fire	
Love is a sea	
Love is a madness	
Love is a gall	
Love is a sweet	

2. Now that you have explored some connotations, will you change your mind about which comparisons are your favorites and which are your least favorites?

3. **CHALLENGE QUESTION (OPTIONAL):** Has Romeo's view of love changed since he listed all the oxymorons? If yes, how? If not, why not?

Create two metaphors for love. To what person, place, or thing would you compare this emotion and experience? Why?

Example: Love is an ocean: warm, playful, and invigorating on the good days, and dark, stormy, and **treacherous** on the bad days.

Glossary:
treacherous: dangerous, risky

Here's What You Need to Do, Romeo . . .

- Read Benvolio's advice to Romeo on how to deal with his frustrating love situation. He recommends that Romeo crash the Capulet ball and compare Rosaline to other women.
- Use your Tips for Tackling the Language handout.

BENVOLIO: Tut, you saw her fair, none else being by,

Herself pois'd with herself in either eye;

But in that crystal scales let there be
  weigh'd

Your lady's love against some other maid

That I will show you shining at this feast,

And she shall scant show well that now

seems best. (lines ___–___)

1. Identify Benvolio's reason for crashing the Capulet party and for having Romeo compare Rosaline to other women. Circle the line(s) where he states his reason.

2. Would you have given Romeo the same advice? Why or why not?

CHALLENGE QUESTION (OPTIONAL): Benvolio uses a metaphor for Romeo's eyes: "crystal scales." What connotations come from *crystal* and *scales*? Do you agree that this metaphor is an **apt** one for *eyes*?

Glossary:
apt: appropriate, fitting

Teaching Romeo and Juliet: *A Differentiated Approach* by Delia DeCourcy, Lyn Fairchild, and Robin Follet © 2007 NCTE.

Shakescholar Close Reader 1.b.2: Scene 1, C

Act 1, Scene 1, Lines _____–_____

From Lord Montague's line, "Who set this ancient quarrel . . .?" to Benvolio's line, "I'll pay that doctrine . . ."

Understanding the Scene
Directions: Familiarize yourself with the following definitions in both figurative language and the history of Elizabethan conventions to help you analyze the end of act 1, scene 1.

> *Metaphor*: a comparison between two unlike things in which one thing is substituted for another. A metaphor is like a math equation, where A = B. For example, we might say to someone, "You're a pig!" Obviously, the person is not actually a pig, but there is one way that the human and the pig can be alike: they both share the qualities of greediness or sloppiness. A metaphor carries more power than a simile because the comparison is stated without calling attention to itself with words such as *like* or *as*, as in a simile.

> *Oxymoron*: the use of paired opposites in a phrase or description. An oxymoron is a situation, place, or thing in which opposites coexist. You see and hear oxymorons all the time: on TV commercials, on restaurant menus, and in political talk. Examples: *jumbo shrimp*, *bittersweet*, *peace force*, *firm pillow*, *alone in a crowd*.

> *Unrequited love*: Look up *unrequited* and complete a definition. Then list any connotations that the word *unrequited* carries as opposed to other synonyms one could use.

> _____

> _____

> *Petrarchan lover*: a person in love with the idea of being in love. Petrarch was an early Renaissance Italian poet known for writing dramatic love poetry; he loved a woman named Laura. They never actually had a relationship. During Shakespeare's time, the ideals of love included these Petrarchan qualities: the lover must be melancholy for the sake of the beloved; the beloved must resist (if not reject) the lover's attentions; the lover must write beautiful poetry to woo the beloved; the lover must suffer from the pangs of unrequited love.

Directions:

1. Read act 1, scene 1, lines _____–_____. Use your Tips for Tackling the Language handout.

2. Answer these questions:

   a. What is Romeo doing that causes his parents to worry?_____

   b. What kind of mood has Romeo been in lately?
   _____

   c. How will Benvolio and the Montagues get to the bottom of the situation?
   _____

The Heart of the Problem: Romeo to Benvolio

1. Romeo plays the Petrarchan poet in this scene. What oxymorons does Romeo use to describe love? List five of the eleven oxymorons he uses below in the pair formation, one opposite on each "side" of each circle. (Ignore the number spaces below for now.)

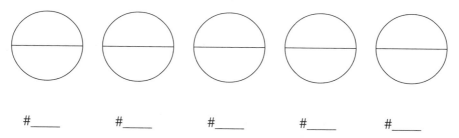

  #_____   #_____   #_____   #_____   #_____

2. Why does Shakespeare choose to have Romeo speak about love using oxymorons? (Hint: what are you as reader learning about Romeo's character and his situation?)

Perfect Opposites

What makes a perfect opposite? Decide what criteria you will use to judge an oxymoron. Then rank five oxymorons that Romeo uses to describe his love for Rosaline. Use a scale of 1 (low) to 5 (high). List criteria below, and rank the oxymorons he uses in the numbered spaces above.

1. _____

2. _____

3. _____

Create three original oxymorons based on your understanding of love.

1._____

2._____

3._____

Why does Romeo use the metaphors of smoke, fire, sea, madness, gall, and a sweet for love?

    1. Pick two of these.

    2. Explain the significance of each comparison

        a. by identifying the connotations (words and images) that would appear in the audience's mind when they heard such figurative language and

        b. by writing a topic sentence that states Romeo's attitude toward love.

METAPHOR   CONNOTATIONS   TOPIC SENTENCE

#1:_____   _____   _____

_____   _____   _____

#2:_____   _____   _____

_____   _____   _____

Create two metaphors for love. To what person, place, or thing would you compare this emotion and experience?
Why?_____

Example: Love is an ocean: temperate, blithe, and vitalizing on the good days, and brooding, tempestuous, and treacherous on the bad days.

1._____

2._____

Lovelorn, Lackluster, Lost . . . That Would Be Romeo

1. Build a case for why Romeo is a Petrarchan lover by quoting two lines below that show his Petrarchan qualities. When you quote a Shakespeare line, include the act number, scene number, and line numbers (see the top of the homework handout for a model). Elaborate beneath each quote with an explanation of how the quote illustrates the Petrarchan ideal.

   a. Quote: _____(___.___.___)

      Commentary: _____

   b. _____(___.___.___)

      Commentary: _____

2. **CHALLENGE QUESTION (OPTIONAL):** Benvolio gives Romeo some advice about how to deal with his frustrating love situation. Would you have given him the same advice? Write a brief monologue in Shakespearean language of what you would say to Romeo in the same situation. Quote Benvolio at least once, either in agreement or disagreement with his advice.

Teaching Romeo and Juliet: *A Differentiated Approach* by Delia DeCourcy, Lyn Fairchild, and Robin Follet © 2007 NCTE.

Lesson 1.c: Vexed in Verona

Student Content and Skill Understandings

See lesson 1.b.

Themes

- Rebellion
- Lust
- Dichotomy and paradox

Materials and Handouts

- 1.c.1: Shakescholar Close Reader, Scene 2, A, B, and C
- 1.c.2: Cue Cards
- (OPTIONAL) Mini-Lesson 3: Girl Power and Arranged Marriage (see page 153)
- 1.c.3: Compacting Fun handout
- Tips for Tackling the Language handout (see page 25)
- Dictionaries and Shakespeare glossary
- Franco Zeffirelli's and Baz Luhrmann's film versions of *Romeo and Juliet*

Activities

STEP 1. WCA: Review of Themes (10 minutes)

Use journals or Socratic discussion questions as anchoring activities to review themes in recent reading.

STEP 2. WCA: TR Questions (15 minutes)

1. OPTIONAL. Teach the mini-lesson on girl power and arranged marriage at the back of the chapter.

2. Review act 1, scene 1, asking students to share with the rest of the class what they translated and discussed with their CRs.

3. Choose questions from A, B, and C handouts so that students of all readiness level have a chance to answer.

STEP 3. WCA: Cinematic Analysis (25 minutes)

1. Watch the Zeffirelli and/or Luhrmann versions of act 1 through the Prince's speech.

2. Ask students which scene plays truer to the text, and ask about the effectiveness of specific directorial choices such as lighting, staging, camera angles, scenery, and props, as well as actors' choices for gesture, intonation, blocking, and articulation. Ask which themes appear most strongly in which version.

STEP 3. OPTIONAL. WCA: Thematic Discussion (5 minutes)

Ask for students to volunteer Tentative Truths: generalizations that seem to sum up what students are seeing in the play concerning social relationships and themes. Use the theme questions on each close reader and any of the following: *What are the root causes of violence in a community? How does a community keep violence in check? How are opposites already coexisting in Verona? Within the characters of Benvolio and Romeo?*

Epilogue: Suggested Homework

1. Give the 1.c.1 Shakescholar CRs A, B, and C and 1.c.2 Cue Cards to students based on readiness level. Mention the importance of finding a quiet place to read aloud on one's own to get comfortable with pronouncing the language, and the importance of having a resource such as a dictionary or glossary on hand.

2. Give the 1.c.3 Compacting Fun handout to eligible students.

Notes on Differentiation

1. This lesson allows for a reflective WCA. Alternating TR, MR, and WCA days is important to maintaining a classroom community while differentiating according to readiness, interest, and learning style.

2. Pay close attention to students' cinematic analysis, as students with strong visual-spatial and even bodily-kinesthetic skills (future filmmakers, actors, producers) might show increased interest, knowledge, and skill.

3. CRs ask students to use cue cards, which are acting prompts for emotions and tones students should take while reading. Reading aloud is a crucial experience and is not only for class; when possible, students must find the time and space at home to sound out Shakespeare's language and imagine the actors speaking it.

4. Note that if you teach the mini-lesson on Elizabethan marriage and parenting, students will be able to answer certain challenge questions on their CRs. Keep an eye out for students who truly stretch themselves with challenge questions.

Shakescholar Close Reader 1.c.1: Scene 2, A

Act 1, Scene 2, Lines _____ – _____

From Lord Capulet's line, "But Montague is bound as well as I . . ." through Lord Capulet's line, "My house and welcome on their pleasure stay."

Understanding the Scene
Materials Needed: Tips for Tackling the Language handout, *Romeo and Juliet*, a dictionary, note-taking materials, and a place where you can read aloud uninterrupted.

Directions:

1. Read the selected lines listed above from act 1, scene 2 between Paris and Capulet.

2. Plot summary: Lord Capulet, Juliet's father, and Paris, a rich man who wishes to marry Juliet, are talking. First Lord Capulet shares how he believes he and Lord Montague, at their age, should be able to "keep the peace." Capulet says that Juliet is probably too young to marry, but if Paris finds Juliet beautiful at the party, and if Juliet likes him, then Paris should **woo** her and "get her heart."

3. Use the Tips for Tackling the Language handout as you read. Stop every six to eight lines and list key words and/ or make literal pictures or symbols in your notes.

4. Read the scene aloud with different emotions for the characters, using the cue cards. Try Paris as insistent and Lord Capulet loving; or Paris loving and Lord Capulet aloof; or Paris solemn and Lord Capulet jovial.

Glossary:
woo: to pursue someone to get them to love you; court

5. Lord Capulet seems like a nice guy. After all, he doesn't seem to be forcing Juliet into an arranged marriage, even though wealthy parents in Shakespeare's day often did. Find three examples from his speech to Paris that prove that Lord Capulet is kind and concerned about his daughter:

    a. _____

   b. _____

   c. _____

6. **CHALLENGE (OPTIONAL):** Is Lord Capulet a typical Elizabethan parent or not?

7. **CHALLENGE (OPTIONAL):** From what you know so far about the play (the title and the action so far), do you think Juliet will have any interest in Paris? Why or why not? _____

_____

8. **CHALLENGE (OPTIONAL):** Write a Top Ten List of Advice to Lord and Lady Capulet on how to be good parents to Juliet. Help them with suggestions as they search for her future husband. Or write the Seven Habits of Highly Effective Suitors for Paris, a bulleted list of advice for courting his love interest, Juliet. Help him with strategies to win her heart.

Shakescholar Close Reader 1.c.1: Scene 2, B

Act 1, Scene 2, Lines _____ – _____

Understanding the Scene

Materials Needed: Tips for Tackling the Language handout, *Romeo and Juliet*, a dictionary, note-taking materials, and a place where you can read aloud uninterrupted.

Directions:

1. Read act 1, scene 2 after reading the plot summary below and the reading comprehension questions you will need to answer.

2. Plot summary: Paris, a noble gentleman of Verona, asks Lord Capulet, Juliet's father, if he can marry Juliet. Lord Capulet says that she is probably too young to marry just yet but invites Paris anyway to the party he is throwing that night. Capulet sends a servant out to remind all the guests about his party. This same servant approaches Romeo and Benvolio for help as they walk down the street since the servant can't read the guest list. Romeo reads aloud Rosaline's name as one of the guests. Romeo is still depressed about his unrequited love for Rosaline, and Benvolio suggests that one way to get over her is to crash this party, see all the other beautiful women, and realize that Rosaline is nothing compared to all the other options out there.

3. Use the Tips for Tackling the Language handout as you read. Stop every six to eight lines and list key words and/ or make symbols in your notes.

4. Read the scene aloud with different emotions for the characters, using the cue cards.

5. Answer *two* of the five character analysis questions below:

    a. Lord Capulet is unique for an Elizabethan father. What is unique about his attitude toward Paris's suit and Juliet's possible marriage? Compare and contrast his attitude with his wife's.

    b. Analyze Paris's statement, "Younger than she are happy mothers made." How does Paris's statement illustrate Elizabethan attitudes?

    c. If Juliet does not like Paris when she sees him and doesn't want to marry him, who would you guess she would she go to for advice? Why?

    d. Romeo is lovesick and depressed, but how does he behave around Benvolio and then the Capulet servant with the invitation to the Capulet's party? Pick some lines that capture his personality at those times.

    e. List all potential outcomes of Benvolio's idea. Do you think it's a good one?

6. **CHALLENGE (OPTIONAL):** Write a brief Director's Memo to a famous actor or actress whom you have cast to play any one of these roles (Romeo, Juliet, Lord Capulet, Lady Capulet, the Nurse, Benvolio, Paris), and discuss what emotion you think should come across most strongly during a particular scene and why.

Shakescholar Close Reader 1.c.1: Scenes 2 and 3, C

Act 1, Scenes 2 and 3

Understanding the Scene

Materials Needed: Tips for Tackling the Language handout, *Romeo and Juliet*, a dictionary, a place where you can read aloud without interruption, and paper or computer for your dialectical journal

Directions:

1. Read act 1, scenes 2 and 3.

2. Using the cue cards, practice reading at least one scene aloud with different voices and emotions for the characters.

3. Which cue card was most effective for a particular character reading and why? (Think like a director of a play or a film or like the actor who has a variety of choices when performing the character.) Write your argument below with a topic sentence and two quotes from the text that prove that emotional choice is best for this character:

TOPIC SENTENCE: _____

_____

QUOTE 1: _____

_____

COMMENTARY:

_____

_____

QUOTE 2: _____

_____

COMMENTARY:

_____

_____

4. Complete a Bard Banter. This dialectical journal is an interpretive journal in which you will record quotations in the left-hand column and comment on their significance in the right-hand column. If you need to better understand the rationale behind such journals, read Mortimer J. Adler's essay "How to Mark a Book," found at http://academics.keene.edu/tmendham/documents/Adler MortimerHowToMarkABook_20060802.pdf. This famous essay explains why we must read closely and actively.

   a. As you read, copy quotations from the play in the left-hand column.

   b. In the right-hand column, let your curiosity, personality, and thoughtfulness emerge. Your goal is to have a dialogue with the text. Write in complete sentences without concern for grammar or spelling. Respond conversationally. This assignment is not an essay, nor is it a question-by-question short answer exercise. Therefore, do not worry about topic sentences and structure. Do write thorough answers that are complete sentences, and do not use numbers, bullets, or fragments.

   c. If some questions contain terms you do not understand, look them up.

Bard Banter

Quotations	Banter
Copy below: ❏ The quotation (just enough text to answer at least four questions and not so much that the quotation is longer than the banter) ❏ The act, scene, and line number in parentheses (an example: 1.4.1–5)	Analyze: (Choose at least four questions to answer, one of which must be the first one.) ▪ How would I translate this quotation into my own words? What are the key words—concrete nouns and powerful verbs? ▪ What questions come to mind as I read this quotation? ▪ What do I think of the characters' choices? Which character intrigues me the most? Why? ▪ What impresses or surprises me about the plot developments here? What do I predict will happen next? ▪ Can I make any personal connections with the story? ▪ Can I make any connections to other literature, historical events, film, or art? ▪ What's the most important issue or theme in this quotation? Are there **motifs**? ▪ What figurative language (simile, metaphor, and hyperbole) do I notice? How does such language emphasize and illustrate the theme? ▪ What words are stressed because of the iambic pentameter and rhyme? How do these metric and rhythmic effects emphasize and illustrate the theme?

Glossary:

motifs: repeated patterns in actions, words, and objects that often call to mind a symbolic image. For example, blood may reappear throughout a story, or violent storms; people may continually use a certain word in dialogue. These images usually connect to larger themes in the story.

Teaching Romeo and Juliet: *A Differentiated Approach* by Delia DeCourcy, Lyn Fairchild, and Robin Follet © 2007 NCTE.

Handout 1.c.2: Cue Cards

Directions:
Use these cue cards as ideas for how to read a character's voice in *Romeo and Juliet*. These suggestions should not only influence your tone of voice, which shows the character's emotions and attitudes, but also

- The volume of your voice (how loudly you read)
- The pace of your voice (how fast or slowly you read)
- The pauses you allow (how you show a character thinking carefully or showing a strong emotion that prevents him or her from speaking right away)
- The emphasis you use (how you choose certain words to emphasize because they are important to the character's mood)
- The gestures and movements you use (how you show a character's physical presence)

If you are using cue cards at home, find a quiet space where you can move around and read aloud using all these techniques.

ALOOF: Read this character in a cold, distant tone of voice, as if you feel disconnected from others or even superior to them.	INSISTENT: Read this character in a pushy, **persistent** tone of voice to get what you want.
IRATE: Read this character in an angry tone of voice, as if you are **fuming** about something.	LOVING: Read this character in an affectionate tone of voice, as if you care deeply for those with whom you are speaking.

SELFISH: Read this character in a childish, demanding tone of voice, as if you deserve all you desire and will become upset if you don't get it.

SOLEMN: Read this character in a serious tone of voice, as if the topic you are discussing is very important, perhaps even **worrisome** or sad.

DEPRESSED: Read this character in a sad tone of voice, as if you have little energy or hope.

JOVIAL: Read this character in a fun-loving, joking tone, as if everything amuses you and you have a positive attitude.

Glossary:
fuming: showing anger and frustration; angry
persistent: the quality of trying even though there are obstacles; not taking "no" for an answer
***worrisome:** troubling, worrying

Other options: FEARFUL, SHY, JEALOUS, CURIOUS, EXCITED

Handout 1.c.3: Compacting Fun: Suggested Activities and Projects

Before you begin working, we will need to discuss

- Which assignments need to be completed and how much choice you will have
- Your work schedule: an estimate of days it will take to complete an assignment
- A rubric for evaluating your work

1. Read ahead on your own and complete a dialectical journal for selected scenes.

2. Complete Close Reader 1.c.1 C for certain scenes as directed by me.

3. Research one or more of the following topics and present this information to the class in a mini-lesson that involves an electronic slideshow, film clips, acting, recitation, demonstration, or models, etc. Make it lively! Topics include (a) the convention of the Prologue and Chorus, Aristotle's definition of *tragedy*, and Shakespeare's five-act structure; (b) fencing and dueling in Renaissance England; (c) marriage customs and gender roles; (d) wet nurses and upper-class families; (e) daily life in London in the late 1500s and early 1600s (even though the play is set in Verona, Italy, the characters represent the Elizabethan culture); (f) Elizabethan Renaissance masquerades, dances, and rituals; and (g) Elizabethan views of Italy; diplomatic relations between Italy and England.

4. Read Romeo and Juliet's first encounter and research the sonnet form to learn more about its history and structure. Scan the lines for the stressed syllables in the iambic pentameter. Prepare a brief essay or oral presentation discussing how rhythm and rhyme emphasize the key themes of the poem and indicate the personalities of the two lovers. Also discuss the significance of the fifteenth line that Romeo speaks, the "extra" in the sonnet. Note: If you choose to present your interpretation orally, consider memorizing and reciting the sonnet for the class. Then write your own sonnet and recite it for the class.

5. Present the 15-minute cut version of the play using the script found at the following URL: http://mainelyshake

speare.com/cutscripts.html. Determine what audience would most appreciate a 15-minute version of the play: the class? younger students? parents and school community? Present the play with conscious choices about acting and blocking, costumes, scenery, music, and other features that demonstrate the larger theme(s). Work cooperatively in a small group, dividing tasks of directing, acting, and design. Choose a scene or act from the play and reduce it to what you feel are the most crucial lines. Use the guidelines found at the following site, http://mainelyshakespeare.com/ShakScCut Guide.doc, to direct your editing choices. Then present the scene, following the same directions listed above.

6. Watch the Zeffirelli and Luhrmann film versions of *Romeo and Juliet* and compare key scenes in terms of camera angles, length of shots, lighting, sound track/ sound effects, and screenplay (the dialogue and directions for actions). After detailing their similarities and differences, argue for effectiveness of directorial/editorial choices in either an essay or a presentation that includes film clips.

7. Storyboard and/or write the screenplay for a modern version of *Romeo and Juliet*. Pick a few key scenes to storyboard or write out in detail. What would be the perfect setting and why? Extra: Which modern actors or actors of a former era would make the best cast and why?

8. Develop a list of questions about characterization, events, themes, and diction. Then, with my assistance, contact a university literature professor or a local community expert for an interview to further probe and discuss the play.

9. Develop a list of questions regarding historical topics of interest relating to the play. Research one topic. With my assistance, contact a college professor, a theater director or actor, or a local community expert for an interview on this topic.

10. The editors of the Arden edition of *Romeo and Juliet* state that the lack of temperance (which can mean lack of "restraint, correctness, and proportion" [61]) is a major

theme of this play. Write an essay that defends the theme of intemperance by finding examples of unbridled appetite and extremity of emotion and action. As you write, consider these questions: (a) Who exhibits unrestrained appetite, emotion, and action? When? (b) Are there characters who contrast as models of restraint? How so and in what situations? (c) How would you suggest these appetites and emotions be tempered?

11. Study a theme throughout the play and present your findings to the class using a creative visual aid, such as a mobile, model, or collage, to represent aspects of the theme and motifs. Talk with me about the difference between a theme and motif so that you can educate your classmates. Make your pictures symbolic rather than literal and be prepared to explain them. Incorporate text quotations into this visual aid as justifications for these symbols.

12. Editors of the Oxford School Shakespeare edition of *Romeo and Juliet* argue that "Mercutio's energetic imagination explodes into life with his fantastic 'Queen Mab' speech. . . . The speech is sheer invention, and must be enjoyed as such—having no deeply significant meaning, and no particular relevance to the action of the play (except to allow enough time for Capulet's guests to eat their supper)" (xvii). Summarize the main argument(s) of several literary critics' analyses of the famous speech of act 1, scene 4. Then write an essay or design a chart or poster in which you present various interpretations. Conclude with a well-defended agreement or disagreement with one or more critics.

13. Literary critic Hildegard Hammerschmidt-Hummel argues that Shakespeare was a closet Catholic. In her reply to a critic available at http://www.uni-tuebingen.de/connotations/index.html, titled "The Most Important Subject That Can Possibly Be," she states that "Shakespeare's plays, especially *Romeo and Juliet* and *Measure for Measure*, are particularly rich in Catholic thought, Catholic rituals, strikingly positive depictions of priests and monks, and invocations of the Virgin Mary and numerous saints. There are many metaphorical references to pilgrimages. Since the nineteenth cen-

tury this has led many scholars to suppose that Shakespeare must have been Catholic." However, it was highly unpopular to be publicly Catholic at such a time in Protestant England. Conduct research of the time period's religious history and the differences between Catholicism and Protestantism using print and electronic media, and read the exchanges between literary critics available at the Connotations website, http://www.uni-tuebingen.de/connotations/index.html. To find this debate, copy Hammerschmidt-Hummel's full name into the search engine available at the Connotations website. Then write your own interpretation arguing whether Shakespeare promotes Catholicism throughout *Romeo and Juliet*.

14. Find famous artistic representations of Romeo and Juliet and compare and contrast the artists' interpretations with the play. Begin your Web research at this URL (http://absoluteshakespeare.com/pictures/romeo_and_juliet.htm) and gather a slideshow collection from the last 400 years of "The Best Art on Romeo and Juliet." Prepare a presentation to the class that explains why these artists have captured the essence of the play.

15. The two lovers marry and the story ends in tragedy. Is this a statement by Shakespeare on marriage? Trace all references to marriage in the play and draw a conclusion. Then study Elizabethan marriage customs as well as English artist William Hogarth's "Marriage à la Mode" (painted more than 100 years after Shakespeare lived). Find the painting at www.library.northwestern.edu/spec/hogarth/Politics.html and research the meaning behind this satirical portrait. Then create your own painting that represents marriage à la mode for Romeo and Juliet's Elizabethan times. Your painting can be literal, figurative, or satirical. Provide a one- to two-page explication of your painting (as museums do) that shares your tracking of marriage references throughout the play and your interpretation of marriage customs.

16. See me for other skill strand assignments.

Act 1, Scene 3

Lesson 1.d: Think of Marriage Now

Student Content and Skill Understandings

- See lessons 1.b and 1.c.

Themes

- Love and marriage
- Rebellion
- Lust
- Dichotomy and paradox

Materials and Handouts

- 1.d.1: Act 1 Journals
- 1.d.2: Shakescholar Close Reader, Scene 3, A, B, and C
- 1.d.3: Shakescholar Close Reader, Scene 4, A, B, and C
- PRO.c.1: Tips for Tackling the Language handout (see page 25)
- Dictionaries and Shakespeare glossary
- Franco Zeffirelli's and Baz Luhrmann's film versions of *Romeo and Juliet*
- (OPTIONAL) performance space (students will be acting scenes)

Activities

STEP 1. OPTIONAL. WCA: Review of Themes and Mini-Lesson (15 minutes)

1. Use an anchoring activity such as journals or Socratic discussion questions to review themes from recent reading.

2. OPTIONAL. Teach the mini-lesson on girl power and arranged marriage (see page 153).

STEP 2. TR Groups: Close Reading of Act 1, Scene 3 (30 minutes)

Distribute 1.d.2 Shakescholar CR, Scene 3, A, B, and C.

Circulate and assist students with following the Tips for Tackling the Language handout.

STEP 3. OPTIONAL. WCA: Cinematic Analysis or Tentative Truths (15 minutes)

1. Watch the Zeffirelli and Luhrmann versions of act 1, scene 3; ask students which scene plays truer to the text and what are the advantages and disadvantages of each directorial choice. How are love and marriage presented in each version? Note: A compacting student pursuing cinematic or literary analysis can lead the class in this activity.

2. Ask students for Tentative Truths. What is most important to Lady Capulet when it comes to marriage? What is most important to the Nurse? What is most important to Juliet? What is significant about our lack of knowledge of Juliet's feelings? Is Shakespeare making any statements about betrothal and marriage in his day?

Epilogue: Suggested Homework

1. Distribute 1.d.3 Shakescholar CR, Scene 4, A, B, and C.
2. Check on the progress of compacting students.

Notes on Differentiation

1. CRs for this lesson require these skills of students: (a) NOV: Use symbols to complete a plot summary of selected lines, answer characterization questions, and predict plot outcomes. Students with visual-spatial learning styles and interests will have an opportunity to shine in the Symbolist role. (b) OT: Use phrases to summarize the plot of selected lines and answer questions that analyze the figurative language of conceit, aspects of characterizations, and predictions of plot outcomes. (c) ADV: Read all of scene 3 and analyze conceit and characterization, predict, and synthesize ideas to form topic sentences expressing character analysis. Eventually, students at all readiness levels will be encouraged to use topic sentences with supporting details. Depending on your students'

readiness levels with writing, you may choose to omit or add such requirements on the A, B, or C handouts.

2. You may decide to spend one period on each CR (1.d.2 and 1.d.3) for the duration of act 1, depending on the rate of your students' comprehension, rather than working on one in class and assigning another for homework. Remember that all of these close reading questions can be used as discussion questions in class. Note that 1.d.3 CRs begin training students to pay close attention to words for their connotations, which leads to developing both topic sentences and commentary, which we call the Quotation Sandwich, the basic core of every paragraph of literary analysis. If students still struggle with free associating on a word, revisit the suggested mini-lesson in Vexed in Verona lesson 1.b. The extra challenge in this stage is to find a theme among the connotations, focus on one, and cite only those connotations that relate to that theme (the adjective).

Handout 1.d.1: Act 1 Journals

Themes of act 1: Love and marriage, rebellion, lust, dichotomy and paradox

1. Familial Love

   - How do the bonds of family demand loyalty? How do such bonds sometimes cause pressure and sacrifice? When should family bonds outweigh true/romantic love bonds?

2. Social Expectations of Love

   - Is true/romantic love possible in an arranged marriage? Why or why not?

   - Can a secret love that a community disapproves of survive? What social barriers do people face in loving each other today? Is there a person of any race, gender, ethnicity, religion, socioeconomic status, or sexual orientation that your parents don't want you to bring home as a friend, boyfriend, or girlfriend? Why?

3. Rebellion

   - Besides the fight that opened the play, where else do you see potential for rebellion? Why? What factors in the play are encouraging if not causing future rebellions?

4. Dichotomy and Paradox

   - Where in the play do you see a person, place, or thing possessing two opposite qualities at the same time? What is interesting about this paradox?

Shakescholar Close Reader 1.d.2: Scene 3, A

Act 1, Scene 3

Understanding the Scene

Facilitator: Reads directions and keeps the group on task. Leads the discussion about what symbol should be used (see Symbolist role).

Reader: Reads the text aloud, stopping when the Explicator asks.

Explicator: Guides group in translating the lines, stopping the Reader every few lines. Everyone should assist the Explicator using the Tips for Tackling the Language handout.

Researcher: Uses the book references, a dictionary, or a glossary to define words that the whole group does not know. Everyone should assist the Researcher.

Symbolist: Designs an easy-to-draw symbol that will help everyone remember the events of the plot up to a certain line.

You will need your Tips for Tackling the Language handout.

To Read:

1. Choose group roles.

2. Open your books to act 1, scene 3, Lady Capulet's line, "Marry, that 'marry' is the very theme . . ." You will stop with Lady Capulet's line, "The valiant Paris seeks you for his love."

3. Listen to the Reader read the first six lines of text.

4. Help the Explicator translate and help the Researcher provide references using your book.

5. Have the Facilitator lead a discussion to propose a symbol for the first six lines.

6. Have the Symbolist design the symbol and everyone copy it on his or her close reader.

7. Proceed through the rest of the text in this manner, explicating and drawing after every sixth line. When you have finished, complete the next steps: To Perform and To Discuss.

Plot summary: Lady Capulet, Juliet's mother, informs Juliet and her Nurse (the woman who breastfed Juliet when she was a baby and who now is Juliet's servant and advisor) that Paris, a noble gentleman of Verona, wishes to marry her.

To Perform:

1. Assign three people to read this scene in the roles of Lady Capulet, Juliet, and the Nurse. Have them pick cue cards and show them to the rest of the group.

   a. For Lady Capulet, use INSISTENT, or ALOOF, or SELFISH.

   b. For Nurse, use LOVING, or JOVIAL, or INSISTENT.

   c. For Juliet, use SOLEMN, DEPRESSED, or IRATE.

2. Read the scene as far as you can and then stop after six to ten lines and discuss whether the cue card direction is working. If it isn't, have the reader pick another card.

3. Read the scene all the way through at least twice, making sure everyone has a chance to read.

4. Now that you've read through the scene trying the different emotions and tones of voice, decide as a group whether you want to make any changes to your scene symbols.

5. If your group is enjoying the scene and has good ideas for blocking and directing it, ask the teacher if you can practice on your feet somewhere to perform it later for the class.

To Discuss:

1. How would you respond if your parent told you that she or he had a person she or he wanted you to marry?

   _____

2. Should parents have a say in a child's marriage?

   _____

In the space below, predict three possible outcomes that could happen in the story, based on this scene:

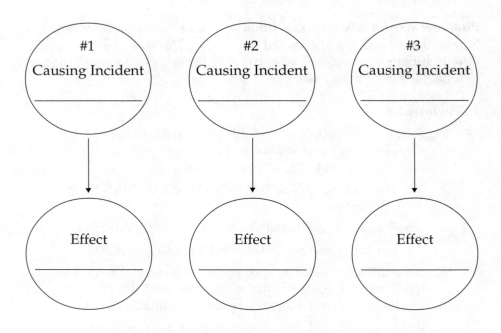

Shakescholar Close Reader 1.d.2: Scene 3, B

Act 1, Scene 3

Understanding the Scene

Facilitator: Reads directions and keeps the group on task.

Reader: Reads the text aloud, stopping when the Explicator asks.

Explicator: Leads group in translating the lines, stopping the Reader every few lines. Everyone should assist the Explicator using the Tips for Tackling the Language handout.

Researcher: Uses the book references, a dictionary, or a glossary to define words that the whole group does not know. Everyone should assist the Researcher.

Summarizer: Leads the discussion about what summary should represent the plot up until the last line discussed; creates a list of words, a brief phrase, or even a topic sentence to summarize the group's agreement on the most important events.

You will need your Tips for Tackling the Language handout.

To Read:

1. Choose group roles and open your books to act 1, scene 3, Lady Capulet's line, "Enough of this . . ." Read to Juliet's line, "Than your consent gives strength to make it fly."

2. Have the Reader read the first six to eight lines of text.

3. Have the Explicator translate and the Researcher provide references. Be sure to use your Tips for Tackling the Language handout.

4. Have the Summarizer lead a discussion about an appropriate set of words or a sentence to represent the plot events up until this line.

5. Once everyone has agreed, copy the summary onto your close reader.

6. Proceed through the rest of the text in this manner, explicating and writing a summary after every sixth line. When you have finished, complete the next steps: To Perform and To Discuss.

Plot summary: Lady Capulet, Juliet's mother, wants Juliet's Nurse to be quiet because the Nurse is telling a long, repetitive story about Juliet falling down and hurting her head as a toddler. At that time, the Nurse's husband, now dead, made a joke with a sexual **innuendo** when Juliet fell on her face, saying that she might be falling on her face now, but when she got older, she would fall backwards (this time with a man). Juliet as a toddler stopped crying and said, "Yes," which the Nurse thought was charming and hilarious. Then Lady Capulet informs Juliet and her Nurse (the woman who breastfed Juliet when she was a baby and who now is Juliet's servant and advisor) that Paris, a noble gentleman of Verona, wishes to marry her.

Glossary:
innuendo: a suggestion or hint

To Perform:

1. Assign three people to read this scene in the roles of Lady Capulet, Juliet, and the Nurse. Have them pick cue cards and show them to the rest of the group.

2. For Lady Capulet, use INSISTENT, or ALOOF, or SELFISH.

3. For the Nurse, use LOVING, or JOVIAL, or INSISTENT.

4. For Juliet, use SOLEMN, DEPRESSED, or IRATE.

5. Read the scene as far as you can and then stop after six to ten lines to discuss whether the cue card direction is working. If it isn't, have the Reader pick another card.

6. Read the scene all the way through at least twice, making sure that everyone has a chance to read.

7. Now that you've read the scene through trying the different emotions and tones of voice, decide as a group whether you want to make any changes to your scene summary.

8. If your group is enjoying the scene and has good ideas for blocking and directing it, ask the teacher if you can practice on your feet somewhere to perform it later for the class.

To Discuss:

1. Lady Capulet uses a conceit to describe Paris. A *conceit* is an extended metaphor, a comparison between unlike

objects or ideas in which the comparison is drawn out for an entire stanza or poem.

    a. Find the conceit. Remember a metaphor is an equation, so find the B. (Paris is the "A" that is equal to this "B." Hint: toward the end you find a more direct statement of A = B.)

    b. Find a quote for each of the four extensions of B,— i.e., which are the different parts or "riffs" that Lady Capulet uses on this metaphor.

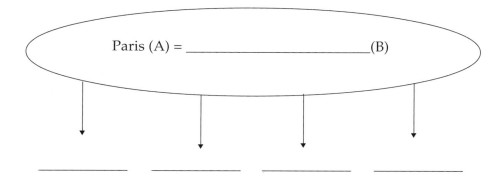

Paris (A) = _____ (B)

2. What might be Lady Capulet's motivations for describing Paris so elaborately? Can you think of more than one reason?

    a. Reason 1: _____

    b. Reason 2: _____

    _____

3. What does such a use of language (conceit) tell you about Lady Capulet's personality? Hint: Look at what she asks Juliet immediately after spending several lines describing Paris. Compare her request of Juliet to what she, Lady Capulet, has just been saying.

    _____

4. How would you respond if your parent told you that she or he had a person she or he wanted you to marry?

    _____

5. What do you think Juliet thinks of her mother's suggestion? Read her last lines *very carefully*.

_____

In the space below, predict three possible outcomes that could happen in the story, based on this scene:

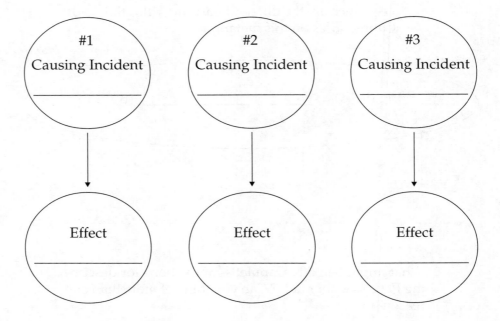

Teaching Romeo and Juliet: *A Differentiated Approach* by Delia DeCourcy, Lyn Fairchild, and Robin Follet © 2007 NCTE.

Shakescholar Close Reader 1.d.2: Scene 3, C

Act 1, Scene 3

Understanding the Scene

To Read and Perform:

1. Choose a Facilitator to read these directions and keep the group on task. You will be rereading all of act 1, scene 3 with a close analytical focus.

2. Assign a Narrator to read the stage directions and any references (including dictionary/glossary) that explain the text.

3. Assign an Explicator, the person who stops the reading every six to ten lines to lead the discussion for translating those six lines into modern language. Use your Tips for Tackling the Language handout. Everyone should assist the Explicator.

4. Assign three people to read this scene in the roles of Lady Capulet, Juliet, and the Nurse. Have them pick cue cards and show them to the rest of the group.

5. Read the scene as far as you can and then stop after six to ten lines to discuss whether the cue card direction is working. If it isn't, have the reader pick another card.

6. Read the scene all the way through at least twice, making sure that everyone has had a chance to read.

7. If your group is enjoying the scene and has good ideas for blocking and directing it, ask the teacher if you can practice on your feet somewhere to perform it later for the class.

To Discuss:

1. Lady Capulet uses a conceit to describe Paris. A *conceit* is an extended metaphor, a comparison between unlike objects or ideas in which the comparison is drawn out for an entire stanza or poem. Find the conceit and star all the extensions of it.

2. Is this conceit effective? What are its advantages and what are its limitations? _____

3. What does the use of an extended metaphor tell you about Lady Capulet's personality?

a. Write a topic sentence to describe her personality—
   what she publicly announces and shows to the world
   about who she is. (These are educated guesses—hy-
   potheses—based on what you have read in the text.
   It's okay if you change your mind later.)

b. Then write a topic sentence of the private thoughts
   she has that she does not share with others.

c. After each topic sentence, write down the line references that serve as evidence for your perceptions of
   Lady Capulet.

4. How would you respond if your parent told you that
   she or he had a person she or he wanted you to marry?
   What do you guess Juliet thinks of her mother's suggestion? Read her last lines carefully. How do you know?
   Where does the subtext (the hidden feelings she does not
   directly admit) shine through?

   a. Decide on topic sentences for both her public per-
      sonality and her private thoughts, and write those
      topic sentences in the spaces available below.

   b. After each topic sentence, write down at least two
      line references that serve as evidence for your per-
      ceptions of Juliet. Write line references in this man-
      ner: 1.3.6 (act 1, scene 3, line 6).

5. Characterize the Nurse. What is her role in this scene?
   What might Shakespeare's purpose be in allowing her to
   tell a lengthy story?

   a. Decide on her topic sentence for her personality.

   b. After the topic sentence, write down the line refer-
      ences that justify your perception of the Nurse.

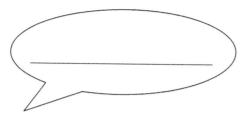

Lady Capulet's Public Personality: A Topic Sentence

Quotations: _____

Lady Capulet's Private Thoughts: A Topic Sentence

Quotations:_____

OPTIONAL: Sketch some symbolic items lying on Lady Capulet's dressing table.

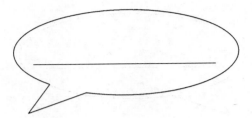

Juliet's Public Personality: A Topic Sentence

Quotations: _____

Juliet's Private Thoughts: A Topic Sentence

Quotations: _____

OPTIONAL: Sketch below some personal objects of value hidden in Juliet's room that no one else has seen.

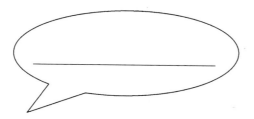

The Nurse's Personality: A Topic Sentence

Quotations: _____

6. **CHALLENGE QUESTION:** Note there is no space to analyze the Nurse's private thoughts. Why might that be?

Teaching Romeo and Juliet: *A Differentiated Approach* by Delia DeCourcy, Lyn Fairchild, and Robin Follet © 2007 NCTE.

Shakescholar Close Reader 1.d.3: Scene 4, A

Act 1, Scene 4

Understanding the Scene

Materials Needed: Tips for Tackling the Language handout, *Romeo and Juliet*, a dictionary, and a place where you can read aloud uninterrupted.

Directions:

1. Read selected lines from act 1, scene 4 starting with Romeo's line, "What, shall this speech be spoke for our excuse?" and ending with Mercutio's line, "Here are the beetle brows shall blush for me."

2. Use the Tips for Tackling the Language handout as you read. Be sure to stop every six to eight lines to circle key words and/or make symbols or other notes in the boxes.

3. Practice reading the scene aloud with different emotions for the characters. Suggestions:

    a. Mercutio, insistent; Romeo and Benvolio, jovial.

    b. Romeo, aloof; Mercutio and Benvolio, insistent.

    c. Romeo, solemn; Mercutio and Benvolio, jovial.

4. Does one choice of tone or emotions work better than another? Why? Write your reasons below.

The tone of "_____" works the best because . . .

_____

_____

CHALLENGE (OPTIONAL): Write a class note, an email, or a U.S. postal service letter to Romeo or Juliet that gives some advice to consider about dating and romantic relationships. Since the lovers are about to meet in the next scene, what should they look for in a new love and romantic partner? How should they be careful? How can they **woo** each other?

Or

Write a Top Ten List of Advice to Lord and Lady Capulet on how they should handle surprise guests who crash their party.

Glossary:
woo: to pursue someone to get them to love you; court

Plot summary: Romeo, Benvolio, and Mercutio, all good friends, are going to follow Benvolio's advice to Romeo by crashing the Capulet party. They are all wearing masks. At that time, a host would welcome anyone in a mask who had prepared a speech that complimented the host and his guests. Romeo is depressed enough to say he's not interested in dancing. Benvolio and Mercutio try to cheer him up. Later, as these friends joke with one another, Romeo confesses that he "dreamt a dream tonight," a dream that told him it wasn't wise to crash the Capulet party. Mercutio claims that the fairy Queen Mab has come to see Romeo since she is the fairy that visits men "as they lie asleep." Then Mercutio begins to describe all the types of people that Queen Mab visits. He is spinning a fantasy of images and jokes that mock different types of people in Elizabethan society.

Directions:

1. Read the description below of one group of people Queen Mab likes to visit, using the references in your book for help on definitions. Important fact to know: Queen Mab is a fairy who drives a **carriage** pulled by tiny creatures, visiting people as they sleep and giving them dreams that are **particular** to the person.

2. Now identify the **connotations** of the italicized words below by filling in the circles for item 3.

   MERCUTIO: Sometime she driveth o'er a *soldier's* neck,
   And then dreams he of *cutting* foreign throats,
   Of breaches, ambuscadoes, and Spanish blades,
   Of healths five fathom deep . . .

Glossary:
carriage: a vehicle with wheels and pulled by horses, usually for people of importance
connotations: associations, implications, and impressions that come to mind when a word is said; not the exact definition but the impression a

word gives. Example: In some cultures, red has a connotation of luck; in others, red has a connotation of anger or violence.

particular: specific

    3. What are the connotations of *cutting* and *soldier*? Hint: begin by using a thesaurus to find synonyms, and then add your own associations.

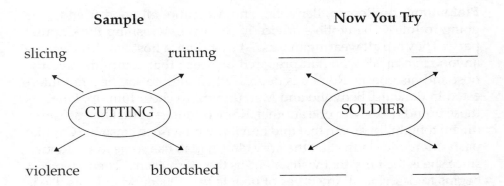

    4. Based on these connotations, what adjective would you use to describe the kind of dreams Queen Mab brings to the soldier? Fill in the blank below.

Queen Mab brings _____ dreams to soldiers.
adjective

(Make sure that the quotation above and the connotations prove this adjective.)

    5. **CHALLENGE (OPTIONAL):** Now write your Quotation Sandwich, which is practice for essay writing we will do later. Fill in the blanks in this paragraph: the topic sentence, the example (quotation), and the commentary.

Quotation Sandwich:

TOPIC SENTENCE: Queen Mab brings _____ dreams to soldiers.
adjective

An example to prove this argument is found in the following quotation,

_____

highlighted section of quote just analyzed

_____. This quotation illustrates the _____
adjective

quality of the dreams because of the following connotations: _____

_____

list of connotations just brainstormed; make sure all

_____

connotations relate to the main adjective

_____

Shakescholar Close Reader 1.d.3: Scene 4, B

Act 1, Scene 4

Understanding the Scene

Materials Needed: Tips for Tackling the Language handout, *Romeo and Juliet*, a dictionary, and a place where you can read aloud uninterrupted.

Directions:

1. Read act 1, scene 4, from the first line through Mercutio's line, "That dreamers often lie." Suggestions:

   a. Mercutio, insistent; Romeo and Benvolio, jovial.

   b. Romeo, aloof; Mercutio and Benvolio, insistent.

   c. Romeo, solemn; Mercutio and Benvolio, jovial.

2. Plot summary: Romeo, Benvolio, and Mercutio, all good friends, are going to follow Benvolio's advice to Romeo by crashing the Capulet party. They are all wearing masks. At that time, a host would welcome anyone in a mask who had prepared a speech that complimented the host and his guests. Romeo is depressed enough to say he's not interested in dancing. Benvolio and especially Mercutio try to cheer him up.

3. Use the Tips for Tackling the Language handout as you read. Be sure to circle key words.

4. Decide which mood that you read suits Romeo's, Mercutio's, and Benvolio's characters the best. Have a quote ready to explain your decision if you are asked to justify your decision in class.

5. Answer *two* of the four following character analysis questions:

   a. How does Romeo's mood change in this scene? Find a line that captures his attitude in the beginning *and* a line that captures his attitude by the end.

   b. What does this mood change tell you about his personality? About his past experiences? About his **intuition**?

   c. Foreshadowing is the use of events, dialogue, and imagery that vaguely or strongly predict later plot events. What events, dialogue, or imagery in this scene might predict a tragedy to come later?

    d. Varying personalities have varying perspectives on love. Compare Mercutio's views of love to Romeo's. What are the crucial differences?

Glossary:

intuition: direct knowledge of the truth of something without using reason or facts; a gut feeling

CHALLENGE 1 (OPTIONAL): A *pun* is a noun meaning "a play on words." There are several ways to pun (also a verb). Think of it as a sport like a spelling bee or the game Scrabble in which you demonstrate your word knowledge.

1. You can use the word multiple times for all its different senses or meanings. (Demonstrate your knowledge of **denotation** and **connotation.**)

2. You can use two similar-sounding words or two words that have similar meanings. (Demonstrate your knowledge of denotation and rhyme.)

3. You can use several words that relate by theme while using a word with multiple meanings. (Demonstrate your knowledge of connotation and theme.) An example: "The wife was so *glad* that her husband was finally taking out the *trash* that she didn't *trash* him for once."

4. You can change a letter or two to create a new word that is a blend of these meanings. For example, *funny + pun = punny*. (Demonstrate your creativity and sense of humor.)

Directions: Fill in the blanks by giving definitions to show all the word-play. Some words will be used for only two definitions; others, for three.

Word	1st meaning	2nd meaning	3rd meaning (optional)
Measure			
Sole			
Bound			
Visor			

CHALLENGE 2 (OPTIONAL):

1. Read Mercutio's Queen Mab speech, which begins with Mercutio saying, "O then I see . . ." and ends with "This is she." Plot summary: Romeo confesses that he "dreamt a dream tonight," a dream that told him it wasn't wise to crash the Capulet party. Mercutio claims that the fairy Queen Mab came to visit while Romeo slept. Then Mercutio begins to describe all the types of people that Queen Mab visits. He is spinning a fantasy of images and jokes that poke fun at different types of people. Queen Mab is a fairy who drives a carriage pulled by tiny creatures, visiting people as they sleep and giving them particular dreams.

2. Identify the connotations of the italicized words below by filling in the circles on this page.

> MERCUTIO: Sometime she driveth o'er a *soldier's* neck,
>
> And then dreams he of *cutting* foreign throats,
>
> Of breaches, ambuscadoes, and Spanish blades,
>
> Of healths five fathom deep...

Glossary:
connotations: associations, implications, and impressions that come to mind when a word is said; not the exact definition but the impression a word gives. Example: In some cultures, red has a connotation of luck; in others, red has a connotation of anger or violence.
denotation: literal or dictionary definition

3. What are the connotations of *cutting* and *soldier*? If you're feeling bold, you can brainstorm the connotations of phrases such as "cutting foreign throats" or "healths five fathoms deep."

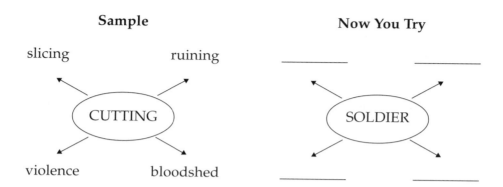

4. Based on these connotations, what adjective would you use to describe the kind of dreams Queen Mab brings to the soldier? Fill in the following blank.

   Queen Mab brings _____ dreams to soldiers.
   adjective

   (Make sure that the quotation above and the connotations prove this adjective.)

5. Now write your Quotation Sandwich, which is a practice paragraph for essay writing we will do later. Fill in the blanks in this paragraph: the topic sentence, the example (the quotation), and the commentary.

Quotation Sandwich:

TOPIC SENTENCE: Queen Mab brings _____ dreams to soldiers.

adjective

An example to prove this argument is found in the following quotation,

_____

highlighted section of quote just analyzed

_____. This quotation illustrates the _____

adjective

quality of the dreams because of the following connotations: _____

_____

list of connotations just brainstormed; make sure all

_____

connotations relate to the main adjective

_____

Shakescholar Close Reader 1.d.3: Scene 4, C

Act 1, Scene 4

Understanding the Scene

Materials Needed: Tips for Tackling the Language handout, *Romeo and Juliet*, a dictionary, a place where you can read aloud uninterrupted, and paper or computer for your dialectical journal.

Directions:

1. Read all of act 1, scene 4.

2. Identify each of the following:

   a. A pun, listing its multiple meanings

   b. Foreshadowing of a tragedy

   c. Romeo's mood swing (one line that captures one mood, and a later line that captures another mood)

3. Practice reading Mercutio's Queen Mab speech aloud with three different voices and emotions for his character: jovial, agitated, and angry. Have fun with the different interpretations.

4. Write a Quotation Sandwich paragraph, which contains the following elements:

   a. A topic sentence that classifies the type of dreams Queen Mab gives the people she visits

   b. Two quotations from the speech to defend your classification

   c. Elaborative commentary on each quotation that cites the connotations of the words used in the quotations illustrating such a classification

5. **CHALLENGE (OPTIONAL):** Complete a Bard Banter (a dialectical journal) that focuses on one or more of the following:

   a. Five key images from the speech that strike you. In the right-hand column, discuss why these images might be of importance to the action or characters in the play.

   b. Five images that you believe set an emotional tone of (choose one) (a) joviality and frivolity, (b) agitation and fear, or (c) anger and violence.

Bard Banter

Quotations	Banter
Copy below: • The quotation (just enough text to answer at least four questions and not so much that the quotation is longer than the banter) • The act, scene, and line number, using arabic numeral notation (for example: 1.4.1–5)	Analyze: (The following questions pulled from the original assignment can help you complete those questions listed previously.) • How would I translate this quotation into my own words? What are the key words—**concrete** or **abstract** nouns and powerful verbs? • What questions come to mind as I read this quotation? • What's the most important theme that I see in this quotation? Are there repeated patterns in actions, words, and objects (motifs)? • What figurative language (simile, metaphor, and hyperbole) do I notice? How does it emphasize the theme? **Glossary:** **abstract:** intangible; a concept or idea. Sometimes abstract nouns have connotations of ideas that can be linked to larger themes. **concrete:** visible, tangible. Sometimes concrete nouns provide images that can be motifs.

Act 1, Scene 5

Lesson 1.e: The Looove Scene

Student Content and Skill Understandings

- Prepare to read and engage with a Shakespeare text: summarize, define, predict, translate, highlight. (AS)
- Prepare for reading a Shakespeare text (summarize, define, predict) and engage with the text (translate, define, highlight). (AS)
- Write a scene using such literary elements as characterization (AS), plot (OT/ADV), theme, setting, tone, and motif (ADV).

Theme

- Love

Materials and Handouts

- Cue cards

Activities

STEP 1. OPTIONAL. WCA and MR: Discussion and Journals (25 minutes)

1. Discussion: Ask students if there is a difference between "love at first sight" and "true romantic love." Are there behaviors that distinguish these two types of love?

2. Journal writing: Ask students to describe the goofiest or most embarrassing way they have seen one teenager ask out another and then describe the most romantic or sweetest way. They may also use their imaginations.

3. MR journal reading: Break the class into MR groups of four. Invite group members to read or paraphrase aloud to their partners what they have written and/ or come up with a list of "Do's" and "Don'ts" for wooing.

4. WCA class discussion: Share any humor, insight, or wisdom gained in the process of making a date or a love connection.

STEP 2. TR or MR Groups: Scriptwriting and Performance (30 minutes)

1. Explain that the class is going to improvise and act, direct, and critique act 1, scene 5 first as writers. Emphasize that today is a theater workshop and not a polished, major performance.

2. Ask students to work in MR groups or TR groups to draft and practice a quick, modern script that shows a guy, Romy, expressing his interest in a girl, Julie. The question the scene must answer is, *How do characters show physical attraction to someone versus emotional, intellectual, and spiritual attraction?* Students should pick either love at first sight or true romantic love as the theme for Romy and Julie. Additional plot complications: Julie's cousin, Ty, hates Romy. Julie's dad, Mr. Cap, has to calm his nephew after Ty sees Romy talking with Julie. Each group needs to write (a) a brief, 4-line speech in which Romy talks to the audience, describing Julie's beauty; (b) a dialogue of approximately 7–10 lines in which Romy woos Julie and Julie responds; and (c) a dialogue between Ty and Mr. Cap of approximately 5–7 lines, showing Mr. Cap trying to control Ty's temper while they observe Romy and Julie in a romantic moment. See Notes on Differentiation for this lesson to understand the differences among TR groups.

STEP 3. OPTIONAL. WCA: Performance (45 minutes)

Have the whole class present, or split the class into two large groups that present to each other. Ask students to comment on how groups have decided to represent love, how characterization or plot evolved and developed, or how a playwright uses a symbol. Consider explaining the differences between theme and motif and symbol if your class as a whole can discuss the finer points. Encourage compliments and constructive criticism of student skits.

Epilogue: Suggested Homework

1. Depending on student readiness, assign for independent reading all or portions of act 1, scene 5 (through Juliet's line, "You kiss by th' book"). Encourage use of Tips for Tackling the Language, note taking, and/or dialectical journals.

2. Check on the progress of compacting students.

Notes on Differentiation

1. For the scriptwriting activity, place students in TR groups so that you can observe students' understanding of characterization, plot, and motif or symbol. Otherwise, use MR groups and allow students to choose which option or level of challenge the group wants to pursue.

   a. NOV, characterization focus: Students should read their script aloud using one or more cue card emotions for each character or suggest their own. They must agree on the most appropriate emotion for each character and practice that version.

   b. OT, characterization and plot focus: Students should (1) show a range of character emotions and personality traits; (2) decide the order of scenes; and (3) create transitions between scenes, such as a narrator or a sound or visual effect.

   c. ADV, characterization, plot, and theme focus: Students should (1) show a range of character emotions and personality traits; (2) write all their dialogues as one scene using transitions; (3) integrate a symbolic object that is passed from Romy, to Julie, to Mr. Cap. (Note: Mr. Cap cannot speak to either Romy or Julie, so think about how he might acquire this symbolic object.)

2. Dialectical journals for homework can be differentiated: NOV students can record and comment on character traits and choices; OT, on character traits and choices and how these affect plot development; and ADV, on how all those elements illustrate theme development.

Lesson 1.f: The Looove Scene Continued

Student Content and Skill Understandings

- Prepare to read and engage with a Shakespeare text: summarize, define, predict, translate, highlight. (AS)
- Summarize plot, identify narrative structure, and explain cause and effect relationships orally and in writing; predict plot outcomes based on narrative structure. (AS)
- Identify and explicate orally and in writing a character's traits using the character's actions, speech, appearance, and reactions from other characters. (AS)
- Use literary terms to articulate interpretations of characters, narrative, and themes: *metaphor, simile, oxymoron* (AS); *blank verse* and *iambic pentameter* (ADV)

Theme

- Love
- Identity

Materials and Handouts:

- PRO.c.1: Tips for Tackling the Language handout (see page 25)
- 1.f.1: Speaking Bardish Close Reader A, B, and C
- Dictionaries and Shakespeare glossary
- Franco Zeffirelli's and Baz Luhrmann's film versions of *Romeo and Juliet*

Activities

STEP 1. OPTIONAL. WCA: Reading and Rehearsal (30 minutes)

1. Explain that the class is now going to explore act 1, scene 5 as readers, actors, directors, and critics. Review the Tips for Tackling the Language handout. Ask students which tips have been most helpful to them in translating Shakespeare's language so far.

2. Begin reading act 1, scene 5 aloud, starting at Romeo's line, "What lady's that which doth enrich the hand . . .?" Stop after reading "For I ne'er saw true beauty . . ."

3. Ask students to give the definition of a simile, metaphor, and hyperbole. Note to students that hyperbole is the use of exaggerated metaphors and similes. Ask the following tiered questions:

   a. NOV/OT: What does Romeo say that Juliet (or her beauty) teaches? What does Romeo really mean?

   b. OT: What kind of comparison is "It seems she hangs upon the cheek of night / As a rich jewel in an Ethiop's ear . . ."?

   c. ADV: What is the significance of this comparison and the others?

      i. Type of comparison: Are any of Romeo's comparisons anything less than hyperbole?

      ii. Reasons for this type: Why would Shakespeare have Romeo speak in hyperbole?

      iii. Theme among the comparisons: Do you see a theme among his comparisons? Where have we seen such romantic comparisons before? Refer back to Romeo's descriptions of Rosaline in scenes 1 and 2 in which he invokes Dian and the sun. Why use figurative language with "light" and "sun" for lovers' talk?

   d. NOV: To what else does Romeo compare Juliet? What is your reaction to such a comparison—is this a very romantic statement? Why? What is true romance? (Ask NOV students to create standards for romance as criteria by which to judge Romeo's approach. It is a good exercise in higher-level thinking skills of evaluation.)

   e. OT: Why does Romeo deny that he has "loved 'til now"?

   f. AS: Do you believe Romeo? How does his description of Juliet compare to some of the student-written descriptions of Juliet in skits the class presented?

g. AS: Is this love at first sight or true love? How do you know?

4. Ask a student to begin reading where Tybalt speaks about Romeo: "This, by his voice . . ." Ask one student to hiss the line, another to whine it, and another to shout it. How does the change in emotional delivery alter our interpretation of character? Of plot? How would the stage need to be set to allow each interpretation?

5. Read through Tybalt's and Lord Capulet's lines, instructing the students to (a) (NOV) remember Tybalt's first scene at the exposition and predict how he will behave here; (b) (NOV) agree on Tybalt's vocal type (is he a hisser, whiner, or shouter?); and (c) (OT/ADV) read Lord Capulet's lines to see the development of emotions (initially jovial and then irate).

6. After Tybalt's line, "Now seeming sweet . . . ," set students an OT activity: to study how Tybalt acts in comparison to his uncle, Lord Capulet. Then compare their Ty with Shakespeare's Ty. Who was whinier? Scarier? Why? Ask students why Shakespeare includes this character at this point in the narrative. What foreshadowing does this imply?

7. Briefly review for students the structure and themes of the sonnet, the ultimate in Elizabethan love poems: its fourteen-line structure, iambic pentameter, and rhyme scheme options, as well as its themes of courtly and sometimes unrequited love. You might also ask ADV students to share their understanding of the Petrarchan lover.

8. Read aloud to students the sonnet exchange between Romeo and Juliet, have a compacting student recite it, or show a cinematic version. Tell students that although they may not understand this sonnet on this first reading or hearing, they soon will.

STEP 2. TR: The Sonnet, or Speaking in Bardish (30 minutes)

1. Separate students into TR groups to explore the sonnet. Distribute the Speaking Bardish CRs A and B & C

to students at their respective readiness levels. Note: Student groups don't have to finish this CR before you bring the whole class together.

2. NOV students may need to review metaphor along with certain vocabulary, and ADV students may need to review irony. You can provide each group with a brief mini-lesson as you circulate to observe and give assistance.

3. OT/ADV: ADV students should complete the challenge questions. They can receive a brief mini-lesson from you on iambic pentameter.

STEP 3. WCA: Reading Comprehension (15 minutes)

1. Ask NOV, then OT, then ADV students to report their translations of Romeo and Juliet's exchange. Ask TR questions from these CRs (1.f.1). Emphasize metaphor.

2. Finish reading act 1, scene 5 aloud and stop to discuss these tiered questions.

   a. OT/ADV: What does Romeo mean when he says, in lines 116–117, "Is she a Capulet? / O dear account! My life is my foe's debt"?

   b. NOV/OT: To say that your life is a debt is a metaphor. What connotation does *debt* have? If Romeo's life has these connotations, what do you predict will happen to his life?

   c. NOV/OT: Juliet uses a metaphor about her grave. Find it. What connotations do *grave* and *wedding bed* have? Why would she say such a thing?

   d. ADV: Why is Juliet's line "My grave is like to be my wedding bed" both ironic and not?

   e. NOV: What does Juliet mean by "My only love sprung from my only hate! / Too early seen unknown, and known too late!"

   f. OT/ADV: What literary element is at work in this same line? Remind students of the skills practiced in scene 4 to identify foreshadowing.

   g. ADV: Juliet uses the word *prodigious*, meaning "ominous" or "foreshadowing evil." Who else has predicted evil forthcoming? When? What is interesting about this parallel?

3. OPTIONAL. Show the complete party scene in the Zeffirelli or Luhrmann movie version.

STEP 4. OPTIONAL. WCA: Tentative Truths (15 minutes)

1. Ask for students to volunteer Tentative Truths, generalizations that seem to sum up what students are seeing thus far about the themes of love and identity. If students struggle, ask them:

   a. What is the play suggesting about how love first begins? About lovers in general?

   b. Is love a reasonable thing? How about hate?

   c. What can we learn about a character through his or her actions? Pick a memorable character in the play and explain how what he or she does (or doesn't do) defines him or her. What can we learn about a character through his or her speech?

   d. How does love or hate create a character's identity? Look specifically at Romeo and Tybalt.

   e. Return to the Pre-Play Poll questions and ask students how they feel at this point about Romeo and Juliet's budding relationship by answering this question: *If you fall in love with someone of whom your family disapproves, should you marry the person regardless of the obstacles?*

2. Ask students to identify the most romantic line from this scene or the most intense moment in scene 5.

Epilogue: Suggested Homework

1. If you give reading quizzes (see ours provided on page 158), you might ask students to review the major events and characters in act 1. Some options for review: have students draw or collage character maps, placing figures on either "side" of Verona, Montague or Capulet; have students review their work on the CRs; have students review any in-text notes (e.g., on stickies) they may have made; let students know that now is the appropriate time

and place to employ study aids, such as print or online notes, since they have already read actively and don't need to reread every single word.

2. Check with compacting students to note their progress on projects.

3. Consider assigning skill strand projects to students throughout a Shakespeare unit instead of at the end, providing a day in class or a night of homework to make progress on a long-term project.

Notes on Differentiation

1. Students refine their close reading skills according to readiness level when you model close reading activities in a WCA, followed by the plot summations and figurative language and/or metrical explorations provided by TRs. Throughout the process, students are encouraged to appreciate the complexity and art of Shakespeare's language.

2. The Speaking Bardish CR provides only two TR levels. Feel free to provide two levels at any time instead of three, since sometimes the distinctions between OT and ADV may be too subtle to require another level of handout. If the B/C level is too much for certain OT students, remember that you can always excerpt these handouts to accommodate your students' needs.

3. Skill strand projects provide differentiation for students by interest and learning style. Integrating these options throughout a unit, whether as modified homework assignments or as long-term projects, helps students invest in and own the experience of reading Shakespeare. Be clear on due dates and end goals. Will each person or group present to the class at a designated time? Will some projects be applied to a larger performance goal? (See, for example, the Director's Promptbook assignment under the creative writing skill strand project list.).

Speaking Bardish Close Reader 1.f.1 A

The Love Sonnet Dissected

Shakespeare has slipped a disguised poem into the middle of his play—a playful yet serious love poem between Romeo and Juliet. This poem is also known as a sonnet.

To help you understand the poem better, please read aloud the following vocabulary.

Profane: (verb) to treat something sacred, holy, or special with abuse. It is also used as an adjective (as in "profane"—bad—language, such as cursing and swearing).

USE THIS WORD IN A SENTENCE:

_____

Shrine: (noun) a place where pilgrims visit to pray to and worship a saint. The pilgrim would request a special favor of the saint through prayer. Usually, a shrine contains a statue of the saint or a relic (a bit of cloth, bone, or even a body part) said to have belonged to the saint.

USE THIS WORD IN A SENTENCE:

_____

Pilgrim: (noun) a person who travels to a shrine or holy place out of devotion to a god or saint.

USE THIS WORD IN A SENTENCE:

_____

Palmer: (noun) a person wearing two crossed palm leaves as a sign of pilgrimage to the Holy Land (what is known today as Israel). In Shakespeare's day, European Christians would make the long journey to the place of Jesus' birth.

USE THIS WORD IN A SENTENCE:

_____

Saint: (noun) a person who had died who was officially recognized by the Catholic Church as holy; Catholics believed (and still believe) that a believer could pray to a saint asking that the saint speak to God on the believer's behalf.

USE THIS WORD IN A SENTENCE:

_____

What idea or image does all of this vocabulary have in common? Make your guess below.

_____

Romeo and Juliet's Love Poem: A Modern Language Summary and Analysis:

ROMEO: If I profane with my unworthiest hand   1

This holy shrine, the gentle sin is this: 2

My lips, two blushing pilgrims, ready stand   3

To smooth that rough touch with a tender kiss. 4

Summary: Romeo decides he wants to kiss Juliet's hand to show her how much he likes her. He takes her hand in his, and he explains that his hand is obviously not as worthy as hers. In fact, she is so worthy, she is like a what? Look at line 2 to find the two words that make the second half of this metaphor, and then write them on the line below.

Metaphor: Juliet is a _____ _____.

Summary: Romeo says that if by touching her he has "profaned" her hand—if he has made it less holy—then he is willing to kiss her hand, to make up for his unworthy touch. Romeo uses a metaphor to describe his lips. What is it? Romeo's lips = _____.
In the second line, Romeo uses a metaphor to describe the kiss he will give Juliet's hand. What two words are the other half of this metaphor? Romeo's kiss on her hand = _____ _____.

JULIET: Good pilgrim, you do wrong your hand too
        much,   5

        Which mannerly devotion shows in this;   6

        For saints have hands that pilgrims' hands do
        touch,   7

        And palm to palm is holy palmers' kiss.

Summary: Juliet accepts the compliment, calling him a new name. What two words does she use to describe him in line 5? _____ _____

Summary: But Juliet isn't going to give in that easily to Romeo or his wordplay. Rather than saying, "No, you can't kiss me," she plays hard to get by saying, "Oh, you've been too mean to your hand by saying it's the 'unworthiest.'" She says that even pilgrims can touch the hands of a saint (imagine a pilgrim rubbing the hand of a statue as he or she prays). In other words, he can touch her hand, and he doesn't have to then kiss her hand to make up for his unworthy touch. Hmmmmmm . . . Does she really want to be kissed?

Our group says (circle one)   YES   NO

Because_____
                Give your group's reason.

Quotation to prove our reason: _____

ROMEO: Have not saints lips, and holy palmers too?   9

JULIET: Ay, pilgrim, lips that they must use in prayer. 10

Summary: Romeo, not to be argued out of kissing Juliet, asks, "Don't saints and pilgrims have lips, too?" She gets the metaphors he's using. Let's review, looking at line 9. Fill in the blanks.

Juliet = _____ and Romeo = _____ _____
(two words)

Summary: Now, if Juliet is what Romeo says she is, then she can't just start kissing him in public after knowing him for only a minute, right?

Plus, isn't her mother probably watching her from across the room to see if she and Paris are flirting? So Juliet responds, "Yes, they have lips, but those lips are meant for *prayer*, rather than smooching." But don't think she's too mad at Romeo . . .

ROMEO: O, then, dear saint, let lips do what hands do;   11

They pray, grant thou, lest faith turn to despair. 12

Summary: Romeo isn't discouraged. He just told us a few minutes ago, when he was talking to himself, that he's never seen true beauty until he saw Juliet this night. If lips are meant for prayer, he argues, then let lips pray the same way that hands pray—in other words, lips get to touch. To drive home his point, Romeo pretends to pray to Juliet, as if she were a saint, saying that if she doesn't let lips pray, they lose their faith—their belief in God—and then they become depressed.

What word does Romeo use in line 12 for depression? _____

JULIET: Saints do not move, though grant for prayers' sake.
                                                    13

Summary: Juliet still hasn't given in to Romeo, not quite. She says, "Sorry, saints don't move, even when they do grant prayers." Here is one of Shakespeare's plays on words, punning, where one word can be used several times in several different meanings.

1. Meaning 1: Define the verb *move* as we use it today. Definition: _____

    _____

2. Now let's use the meaning you just found and apply it to saints from Elizabethan times. Why can't saints "move"? (Go back to the original definition of *saint*. If a pilgrim went to a church in 1594, would he or she get to see the saint, alive and in person? Why not?)

    _____

    _____

3. Meaning 2: In Shakespeare's day (and today), *move* could also be a verb that meant "to start something." Today

you might hear a person who works in government say in a meeting, "I move that we vote now," but the average person doesn't tend to use the word this way. We might instead say, "I suggest that" or "I vote that . . ." So, back in Shakespeare's day, Juliet is saying how saints don't "move," or suggest something to pilgrims. It's the pilgrim who has to come to a saint with a suggestion, which is the pilgrim's prayer.

Summary: But look at the second half of Juliet's sentence. She gives Romeo an opening! She says saints can do what instead?_____
_____. In other words, saints might not start the prayer, but once the pilgrim has prayed to the saint, the saint gives pilgrims what they are requesting. So if Romeo is praying at this holy saint's shrine (Juliet), this saint might just grant his prayer.

ROMEO: Then move not, while my prayer's effect I take.

14

Summary: Romeo uses definition number 2 of *move*. He moves in to do what? (Hint: Why does he ask Juliet to stand still? What's he hoping to do the whole time he's wooing her?

Now the love poem is over, but Romeo adds one more line. Translate it into your own words. Look up any words you need to in the dictionary—and remember what he's just done. (Hint: go back to line 2.)

ROMEO: Thus from my lips, by thine, my sin is purg'd. 15

Teaching Romeo and Juliet: *A Differentiated Approach* by Delia DeCourcy, Lyn Fairchild, and Robin Follet © 2007 NCTE.

Handout 1.f.1: Speaking Bardish B & C

The Love Sonnet Dissected

Shakespeare has slipped a disguised poem into the middle of his play—a playful yet serious love poem between Romeo and Juliet. These lines **constitute** a sonnet, a type of poem that has fourteen lines, is written in iambic pentameter, and follows a specific rhyme scheme. To understand this poem, you should know the following vocabulary words. Define them using a dictionary or the play's reference notes, and use each in a sentence. Bonus: put all sentences in one story.

Profane (verb):

_____

Shrine (noun):

_____

Pilgrim (noun):

_____

Palmer (noun):

_____

Saint (noun):

_____

Answer the questions about the sonnet, **transcribed** below.

Glossary:
constitute: make up; create
transcribed: copied

ROMEO: If I profane with my unworthiest hand   1

    This holy shrine, the gentle sin is this: 2

    My lips, two blushing pilgrims, ready stand   3

    To smooth that rough touch with a tender kiss. 4

1. Who or what is Romeo comparing to a shrine?_____
2. How is he "profaning" that shrine? (Note: stage directions are hinted at in the lines.)_____

3. How does he propose to **make amends** for his "profane" action? _____

Glossary:
make amends: make up for; apologize

JULIET: Good pilgrim, you do wrong your hand too much,
                                                              5

Which mannerly devotion shows in this;   6

For saints have hands that pilgrims' hands do touch,   7

And palm to palm is holy palmers' kiss.   8

Will Juliet allow Romeo to kiss her with his lips? Support your answer by quoting the text._____

_____

CHALLENGE QUESTION (OPTIONAL): Does Juliet really want to be kissed? Offer proof for your answer by quoting the text and elaborating on it.

QUOTE:

_____

_____

COMMENTARY:

_____

_____

What does she say that saints and palmers use to "kiss"?_____

ROMEO: Have not saints lips, and holy palmers too?   9
JULIET: Ay, pilgrim, lips that they must use in prayer. 10

Why does Romeo ask if saints and palmers have lips?

_____

Translate Juliet's response.

_____

CHALLENGE QUESTION: What is the **subtext** of Juliet's statement— what emotions is she hinting at? Why is she hinting rather than saying what she means directly? Offer proof from the text that gives the hints and then her reasons for not being direct. Hint: what else could she be saying?

_____

_____

Glossary:
subtext: the hidden meaning; the words that she is feeling but not saying

ROMEO: O, then, dear saint, let lips do what hands do; 11

  They pray, grant thou, lest faith turn to despair.
                                                    12

According to Romeo, why should lips be allowed to kiss?_____

JULIET: Saints do not move, though grant for prayers' sake.
                                                    13
ROMEO: Then move not, while my prayer's effect I take.
                                                    14

What is the pun in these lines? (Hint: find the repeated word used with more than one meaning.)

_____

CHALLENGE QUESTIONS:

1. Is Juliet saying that she will or will not grant Romeo's request for a kiss? Offer proof.

   _____

2. How does Romeo's description of Juliet relate to Petrarchan love? How is the situation that they are in not very Petrarchan?

   _____

3. Are Romeo's actions here surprising or typical? What has act 1 shown you about his character?

_____

4. Write the stage directions (blocking and gestures) for each character during each line. _____

_____

_____

_____

_____

5. Why might Shakespeare rely on so many religious metaphors in this scene? What themes might he be be trying to show us? _____

_____

_____

6. Using what you know of iambic pentameter, scan the lines. What words are emphasized?

Teaching Romeo and Juliet: *A Differentiated Approach* by Delia DeCourcy, Lyn Fairchild, and Robin Follet © 2007 NCTE.

Skill Strands

Creative Writing

Identity Poem: Bob, Bob, Wherefore Art Thou, Bob?

In *Romeo and Juliet*, one of the major themes is identity. Consider some of the issues that Juliet and Romeo think about when they try to explain who they are: how their actions define them, how others define them, and how their loves define them.

Write a poem that captures your identity. Follow these guidelines:

Lines 1–2: Describe one action you associate with yourself. For example: *Dropping basketballs through the hoop , / The net swishing and dancing.*

Lines 3–4: Describe a second action that you associate with yourself, but one that is not necessarily related to the first action. For example: *Strumming my guitar.*

Lines 5–6: Describe a third action related to yourself. For example: *Arguing with my brother over fantasy football.*

Line 7: State your name, followed by an epithet, which is a short way of describing yourself. For example: *Bob Bobbert, Cartoonist Extraordinaire.*

Lines 8–10: List five names you apply to yourself or that others apply to you—actual names, plus roles—student, sister, friend, teammate, grandkid, etc.

Lines 11–13: List and briefly describe at least three people you care about.

Lines 14–16: List and briefly describe at least two things you care about.

Lines 17–19: Briefly repeat the actions mentioned in the first six lines.

Consider writing a similar poem for your favorite character thus far in *Romeo and Juliet*.

Dramatic Performance

Stage Setting for Act 1, Scene 1

Block act 1, scene 1 (Sampson through the Prince's command for all men to depart) in one of five ways: (1) with a promptbook (for verbal-linguistic learners); (2) with a sketch of a stage scene or with storyboards (visual-spatial); (3) with a written/visual justification of Hollywood celebrities (interpersonal, verbal-linguistic, and visual-spatial); (4) with percussive, wind, and other instruments and/or recorded music (musical); or (5) with your bodies (bodily-kinesthetic).

Soliloquy Memorization

Memorize a soliloquy from act 1 and present it with attention to iambic pentameter, correct pronunciation, articulation, pacing, and volume. Seek coaching from someone with drama experience.

Director's Promptbook

Create a director's promptbook for any scene from act 1. This is the book that helps a director decide on what choices actors should make to perform the play.

1. Analyze character traits by studying the scene text in order to direct actors' choices for sound (emphasis, volume, pacing) and movement (gesture, posture and stance, blocking).

2. Write specific stage directions onto a photocopied version of one scene.

3. Write brief paragraphs ("A Note to the Actor Playing Romeo," and so forth) as if you are a director of a scene to give general guidelines about the performance of these characters. Actors need themes, or big ideas, to follow; otherwise you're just giving them lots of little tasks. Use adjectives and nouns to describe how you see a character's personality (a topic sentence!) and then provide supporting details from the text to show why the actor should perform it this way.

Setting Adaptation

Rewrite scene 1 of act 1 by setting it in your hometown or city. Adapt the language and actions of the characters to the cultural traits and themes of our historical era as well as your community's culture, and revise the script accordingly.

Performance

Present any scene with conscious choices about acting/blocking, costumes, scenery, music, and other features that demonstrate the larger theme(s). Work cooperatively in a small group, dividing tasks of directing, acting, and design.

Performance of 15-Minute Romeo and Juliet

Present the 15-minute cut version of the play using the script found at the following link: http://mainelyshakespeare.com/cutscripts.html. Determine what audience would most appreciate a 15-minute version of the play: the class? younger students? parents and school community? Present the play with conscious choices about acting/blocking, costumes, scenery, music, and other features that demonstrate the larger theme(s). Work cooperatively in a small group, dividing tasks of directing, acting, and design.

Shakespeak

You're about to dive into Shakespeare's land where the beginnings of modern English as we know it first appeared in print. Let's school ourselves in some phrases. Directions: (1) form a group of two or more students (no more than four); (2) review Elizabethan words and phrases listed below with your partner(s); (3) write a brief skit of two minutes or less in which two or more people argue and get in a fight, using as many Elizabethan words and phrases as you can; (4) bonus: refer to themes if you can; (5) practice it in preparation to show the whole class.

Elizabethan Word or Phrase	Modern Translation
to carry coals	to be insulted
And	can mean "and" in our modern meaning or "if" in other contexts
Draw	pull out a weapon (a sword in Elizabethan times)
Ay	yes
Nay	no

to be moved	to be provoked or emotionally engaged
Stand	stick around and act with confidence and bravery, as in "stand your ground" for a fight
Thee	you
Thy	your
'tis	abbreviation of "it is"
take the wall of any man	show yourself to be better than or superior to someone else (in Elizabethan times, it was safer to be a pedestrian who stuck to the wall; remember why?)
'tis all one	"it doesn't matter"
Wilt	will (as in the verb, "You will . . .")
Hadst	would or had
Quarrel	argue or start a fight
let us take the law of our sides	let's follow the law (rather than breaking it)
let them take it as they list	let them take it as they like (react or interpret as they want to)

Cinema

In Fair Verona Where We Lay Our Scene: Establishing the Cinematic World

Baz Luhrmann's modernized version of *Romeo and Juliet* (*Romeo + Juliet*) sets the play in Verona Beach (sounds a lot like Venice Beach, California), which is a hot, sexy city where gunslingers **abound**. Ladies in bikinis, expensive cars, palm trees, and bright colors flash across the screen. The Prologue is delivered via a news anchorwoman on a television set. If you were setting the scene for your own film version of *Romeo and Juliet*, how would you do it?

Glossary:
abound: appear in great number

1. Watch the first ten minutes of Luhrmann's film to examine how he establishes a visual world.

2. Create a poster called "The Cinematic Prologue" in which you establish the visual tone or cinematic texture of your film.

   a. Establish the time period and setting of your film.

   b. Who will deliver the Prologue? A man selling newspapers on the corner in 1920s New York City? A scrolling text à la *Star Wars* with a fictitious planet and the cosmos swirling in the background?

3. Provide colors and images in a collage arrangement to make clear to your audience what to expect once this film hits the theaters. What is the visual "feel" you are going for?

4. Casting call: Decide which famous actors will play which parts. Use the list of characters at the front of your playscript as a reference, and include a complete cast list on the back of your poster.

Socratic Discussion

For a Socratic seminar discussion to be a success, students must understand that the conversation rests entirely on their shoulders. The teacher's role is to keep questioning alive, to encourage students to return to the text to quote evidence and elaborate on it, and to eventually become an outside observer. The students must speak to one another and not the teacher. Establish and review the ground rules with students before the discussion, and have the students prepare notes on the seminar questions in class or for homework (see the list of possible act 1 questions on pages 145–47). Have speakers sit in a circle or U shape, observers on the outside.

Some students like speaking in generalizations, while others like speaking in specifics. Whatever a student's preference, all must learn to quote the text to defend an argument. Ask students to bring their notes and texts to each discussion.

Suggested Ground Rules

- Respect all participants. Disagree with grace, understanding, and courtesy.

- Participate selectively if you have a lot to say. Draw others into the discussion.
- Listen actively by watching and refraining from distractions and side conversations.
- Build on points previously made when you make your point.
- Wait to speak until your peer is finished.
- Back up your points with textual evidence.
- Evaluate your peers with constructive criticism (see the following Socratic Seminar Peer/Teacher Evaluation).

Speaker_____   Observer_____

Socratic Seminar Peer/Teacher Evaluation

Date _____   Theme(s) _____

Behaviors	Excellent	Good	Fair	Needs Improvement
Shares the discussion rather than monopolizing or interrupting				
Listens to others by building on points previously made				
Offers comments that extend discussion; raises new points; asks clarifying questions; and/or examines the logic of ideas				
Provides relevant supporting evidence from the text				
Respectfully disagrees				
Speaks loudly and clearly				
Provides relevant, appropriate, and respectful real-life examples				

Comments:

Possible Formats for Socratic Seminars

- *TR differentiation*: NOV, OT, and ADV groups can discuss separately in TR groups of seven to ten students, or groups can be matched to observe and evaluate each other (fish bowl style) and then switch. Assign different questions to each group to create the richest discussion later when the class regroups as a whole and so that each group has original ideas to share. TR questions appear throughout a Socratic seminar, with relevance questions being more NOV-friendly. Also consider "chunking" discussion into 25-minute experiences for students with less experience and maturity until they grow more comfortable with the guidelines. You can teach a remediation mini-lesson in a particular skill area to an NOV group that needs review of topic sentences, figurative language, and other concepts while the other TR groups run their own discussions; then follow the NOV lesson with a brief Socratic discussion. NOV students may also need more supervision and support in learning discussion skills and ground rules. With the following acts in the play, you can increase the amount of time for discussion as students increase in skill level.

- *MR differentiation*: Split the OT group in half and combine half with the ADV group and the other half with the NOV group. The two combined groups evaluate each other.

- *WCA*: Have all students address the selected questions in a WCA seminar. Benefits of this format include students observing and building on one another's strengths, such as the variety of rich perspectives: students with street-smart, practical wisdom might educate those with more sheltered, abstract perspectives; those more linguistic can model a love of close reading, debate, and language for less avid readers. Possible drawbacks include intimidation of students not comfortable with reading and discussion or of those gifted in reading and speaking embarrassed to be perceived as "intellectual."

- A note about compacting students: Tell these students and any others who have read ahead that they should refer only to act 1's text and refrain from giving spoilers. Even though students should all know that the end is tragic, it's not helpful to have a compacting student or any ADV reader "hold forth" and show off knowledge that others cannot dialogue with. While knowing how the play turns out is an advantage, these students can still benefit from sharing with their peers in intensive study of act 1 and quoting relevant textual evidence. If possible, determine before a student compacts what level of skill he or she possesses in Socratic discussion by giving a quick oral exam using a few of the play-related and relevance questions on a passage; the student's performance will tell you how much she or he can gain from WCA or TR discussions.

Act 1 Socratic Seminar Questions

Play-related questions are "local" queries, ones that target character, plot, and theme, while relevance questions are "global" queries that target student experiences as they relate to the big questions of the play. Relevance questions should always be discussed with the standard of evidence (provide appropriate anecdotes and examples from real life) and with the goal of bringing the conversation back to the play.

Love and Marriage: **Play-Related Questions**

- Are Romeo and Juliet experiencing true love? If not, explain what you believe they are experiencing. If so, explain what you believe their course of action should be.
- How high is the pedestal Romeo creates for Juliet? Does she deserve this?

Love and Marriage: **Relevance Questions**

- How do you define true love?
- Why do people put a beloved person on a pedestal?
- Marriages in Western societies tend to be based on romantic love, but during the Elizabethan era they were based on economics, family politics, and social status. Which approach fits your values and beliefs? Why? What are the arguments for both?

Rebellion: **Play-Related Questions**

- The word *rebellion* is often associated with violence, yet Romeo and Juliet are rebellious through their love. Discuss the forces and authorities they are rebelling against.
- Do you think nonviolent resistance will be Romeo's and Juliet's choice in order to be together? What would nonviolent resistance look like in their situation? How do you know they would or would not choose this route? What would be a violent way of achieving their goal to be together?

Rebellion: **Relevance Question**

- What are some of the situations today and in history when nonviolent resistance has been effective?

Fate: **Play-Related Questions**

- Romeo has a premonition that he will die an early death if he goes to the Capulet party, but he goes any way. Why does Romeo make such a choice?
- Juliet declares that if Romeo is married, her grave will be her wedding bed. We know he's not married, but is her statement fateful?
- Do Romeo and Juliet seem in control of their lives thus far, or is something else controlling them?

Fate: **Relevance Questions**

- Do you believe in fate? Can people who believe in fate change their fate?

Identity: **Play-Related Questions**

- How do others define Juliet's identity? How does she define herself?
- How do others define Romeo's identity? How does he define himself?
- Are Romeo and Juliet missing opportunities for self-definition that you have as a modern teen?

Identity: Relevance Questions

- What are the elements that constitute a modern American teen's identity?
- Are you missing opportunities for self-definition that Romeo and Juliet have?

Motifs: Play-Related Questions

- Masks: What is the symbolic significance of the masked ball at which the lovers meet? How are they "masked"? By what? By whom? To whom? How are they "unmasked"?
- Do you predict more masking or unmasking to occur for these lovers?

Motifs: Relevance Questions

- Masks: Consider the different masks people wear in everyday society. Why do we wear them? When? What determines the masks we choose? Are we ever completely unmasked?

Mini-Lessons

Mini-lessons can be presented with your explanations (lecture notes) and directions (notes to students on how to take notes or complete handouts). Consider adding visuals and electronic slideshows to enhance these presentations, or asking a compacting student to present these notes with researched additions.

Mini-Lesson 1: The Shakespearean Sonnet

Explanations: The Prologue of *Romeo and Juliet* employs sonnet form. While there are many different types of this poetic form, Shakespeare wrote so many sonnets (154 to be exact) that he has his own version of the form named after him. The chief subject of his sonnets was usually romantic love. So why put one at the beginning of *Romeo and Juliet* that gives away the entire plot? (a) Shakespeare's audience would already have been familiar with the plot of this relatively common tale. Shakespeare wasn't really giving away any secrets or providing a spoiler. (b) The Prologue warned the Elizabethan audience that the play was about to begin by having the Chorus (a single person) come out on stage. (c) The Prologue also quieted the groundlings, the poorer people who paid less to stand and mill about in the Globe Theatre's Yard right at the front of the stage and who were more than likely already a bit rowdy.

Directions: Look at the Prologue with a partner. How many lines does it contain? If you were going to break down the Prologue into stanzas (a section of lines from a poem that stands apart from other sections, often four lines or more), where would you put the breaks? Pay close attention to punctuation as you consider these questions.

Explanations: Shakespearean sonnets break down into three quatrains (four-line stanzas) and a final couplet: fourteen lines in all.

Directions: With your partner, look at the last word in each line of the Prologue. What is the rhyme scheme of this fourteen-line poem?

Explanations: The rhyme scheme of any poem can be indicated using letters. The Shakespearean sonnet rhyme scheme is always abab, cdcd, efef, gg.

Directions: Count the number of syllables in the first and second lines of the Prologue.

Explanations: Sonnets are written using iambic pentameter. This meter employs ten syllables per line. Every second syllable is stressed. This way of writing reflects the natural rhythm of the human heartbeat as well as the rhythm common to our way of speaking.

Directions: Break the first line of the Prologue into five sets of syllable pairs. Put a U over the first syllable (the unstressed syllable) and a / over the second syllable (the stressed syllable) in each pair. Read the line out loud, putting slightly more emphasis on the stressed syllables.

Further Directions: Speak the following lines of iambic pentameter as you normally would, noting where you put the stress. Then break down the lines into five pairs of unstressed and stressed syllables. Try again, this time changing the pattern around where you think you need changes; if you think the first syllable should be stressed rather than the second, explain why. Sometimes Shakespeare breaks his rhythm to make a point. What point would you be making if you broke the pattern?

> I miss him more than usual today.
>
> I know the way to go is over there.

Handout PRO.c.3: Notes on the Shakespearean Sonnet

Name _____ Period _____ Date_____

Why start with a sonnet?
Shakespeare began the play with a sonnet that explains the events of
the play because:

        1._____

        2._____

        3._____

How many QUATRAINS (4-line stanzas)?_____

How many COUPLETS (2-line stanzas)?_____

Total number of lines in a sonnet =_____

What's in a RHYME? a, b, c, d, e, f, g

Use the letters above to show the rhyme scheme of a Shakespearean
sonnet.

Divide each line into five syllable pairs.

       Two households, both alike in dignity

       In fair Verona, where we lay our scene

Iambic pentameter =

_____ syllables per line

_____ pairs

Each pair begins with an _____ syllable

and ends with a _____ syllable.

In the first two lines of the Prologue, mark the unstressed syllables with a U.

Mark the stressed syllables with a /.

Do the same divisions and stress marking on the following two sentences.

> I miss him more than usual today.

> I know the way to go is over there.

Teaching Romeo and Juliet: *A Differentiated Approach* by Delia DeCourcy, Lyn Fairchild, and Robin Follet © 2007 NCTE.

Mini-Lesson 2: Would You Believe What They Did Back Then?

Explanations: You're walking down an Elizabethan street in London, England. It's 1594. You see some not-so-savory sights, smell some not-so-savory scents, and avoid a not-so-savory accident. The streets are full of trash and horse droppings: they work like open sewers. Remember, there are no toilets or sewer systems. All kinds of filth and human waste are running through the streets down to the Thames River. Watch your step and stay close to the wall! If you stick close to the wall, you won't dirty your shoes as much, and you won't get waste dropped on your head from a window above. If you happen to be rich and of the nobility, you have the right to walk closest to the wall (Weller par 6). Unfortunately, you're a poor servant or working class, like a good deal of the English population at the time. You have to step aside and give up the wall when a "superior" person passes.

Directions: Draw or write the key words or images I just explained. What did you choose to write or draw?

Explanations: You're lucky to have avoided a nasty encounter with refuse, but uh-oh, there's trouble on the horizon. Just ahead of you are two guys coming your way. They're carrying bucklers, small, round shields sporting the insignia of their bosses (Weller par 1). What do people wear today on the street that would be the equivalent of a buckler?

Explanations: And what's worse, they're wearing livery, i.e., a uniform of the master they work for—head of a family that is enemies with your master! Not good. Okay, now things are bad as can be, because as they approach, you see they carry swords, which usually only gentlemen—the superiors—wear (Weller par 1)! These guys are looking for trouble.

Directions: Draw a symbol for the Capulet or Montague family buckler.

Explanations: The trouble these guys are looking for will probably happen at a place called Smithfield, also known as Ruffians Hall, where men looking to duel meet (Levenson par 5). You don't want to tangle with these guys, so dart into a doorway and make yourself inconspicuous. They pass you. You breathe a sigh of relief. All this fear has made you hungry, so you head for the market, where you scout for some lunch. Too bad you don't have much money; looks like you'll have to settle for Poor-John, named because it's quite a deal—the cheapest dried fish.

You get the tail, the head, the whole fish, but it's so dry that it's hard as wood (Weller par 7). Hah, here's your weapon! Now you're safe. You pay the fishwife at the stall and gnaw away at your lunch, trying not to break a tooth.

Directions: Draw an image or write some notes to summarize what you just learned.

Explanations: Uh-oh, here come those guys again. They weren't headed to Ruffians Hall; they must have come up another street to the market. Hey, they're mocking you and your pitiful lunch. You pretend not to see them until—wait, no, wait, yes, they really are biting their thumb at you! That's beyond rude—that's a challenge! Biting your thumb at someone is like giving the fig. If you give the fig, you move your thumb in and out between your index and middle finger. Just guess how that gesture could be interpreted as obscene and therefore insulting. No, don't try it. So, though biting the thumb isn't quite "the fig," it's still saying the same thing, and you do it like this: put your thumbnail just behind your top teeth. Now flick your thumb toward the other person so that you make a cracking sound. You just "bit your thumb" at someone, Elizabethan style (Weller par 10). Do not do this here, in the hallways, or at home!

Directions: Write two sentences that explain how Elizabethans were in one way just like us and in another way not like us at all.

Mini-Lesson 3: Girl Power and Arranged Marriage

Explanations: It's 1594 again, and you're a girl growing up in Elizabethan England, about Juliet's age of thirteen. It doesn't matter how old you'll get: you'll never be guaranteed a chance to go to school, to get a job, to vote, or to have many, if any, legal rights. But the leader of England—one of the wealthiest, most successful countries in the modern European world—is female: Queen Elizabeth I! How can a woman rule the nation while all other women have next to no rights (Papp & Kirkland 68)?

Directions: Discuss with a partner or a triad how Elizabethans could justify such a paradox, which is two opposites coexisting at once (but not necessarily a two-word pairing like an oxymoron), and live with it.

Explanations: In *Romeo and Juliet*, Lord Capulet seems to be a modern Renaissance father, perhaps even on the cutting edge of women's rights, in his desire for Juliet to be in love with the man she marries. He tells

Count Paris he must win Juliet's heart and that she is too young to marry just yet. Yet the old-fashioned social rules of the time surrounding arranged marriage in Elizabethan England are quickly enforced once Lord Capulet has a change of heart and gives his word to Paris that the nobleman shall indeed wed Juliet, because "I think she will be rul'd / In all respects by me; nay, more, I doubt it not" (3.4.13–14). So just what were the rules of the day on arranged marriage?

Arranging the Marriage

- Not all marriages during the Elizabethan era were arranged. Arranged marriage was much more common among the upper classes, though the medieval church reminded parents to consider their children's wishes when it came to such unions (Griffin).

- Christian doctrine viewed the purpose of marriage as threefold: comfort and support for husband and wife, procreation, and regulation of sexual activity (Griffin).

- Among prosperous families like the Montagues and Capulets, marriage was perceived as a means of gaining wealth, land, allies, and power. The jointure through marriage of two noble families was considered smart both financially and politically (Griffin).

- Often, arranged marriages were determined when the children were quite young.

- Fathers or male relatives of girls of the nobility selected the husbands.

Directions: Draw or write on your sheet what you have just heard. What symbols, words, and phrases work best to summarize this information?

- In Elizabethan England, there was no legal marrying age, but the typical age began at about fourteen. Because life expectancy was shorter, women began having children at a younger age during this era (Crispen).

- However, men of lower socioeconomic status were discouraged from marriage by apprenticeships that sometimes lasted seven years. In an overpopulated nation, many couples waited to marry into their twenties, and by that time, often the bride was pregnant (Papp & Kirkland 96–97).

- It was no shame to be a pregnant bride, since Elizabethans considered an engagement, or betrothal, to be as good as marriage. However, it was a great shame to be pregnant and remain unmarried. Then the woman was in danger of being dishonored, and her child without a father would be considered a bastard, a shameful state of affairs (Papp & Kirkland 97).

Directions: Draw or write what you have just heard on your sheet. What symbols, words, and phrases work best to summarize this information?

Dowry and Economic Protection for the Wife

- The dowry, or marriage portion, consisted of the money, riches, and property the woman brought to the marriage (Crispen).

- The precontract, or betrothal, protected the woman by containing a clause laying out the dower rights. This was an agreed upon amount for the wife's living expenses in the event that she was widowed. Yet this money was given to the widow only if she did not remarry or failed to return to her father's house (Crispen).

- Because of their inferior place in society, Elizabethan women could not inherit property or wealth no matter where they fell in the birth order. Control of family wealth was passed to a son or the father's brother if necessary ("Life in Elizabethan England").

- Women lost all rights to their dowry once they were married. Even if a woman married "beneath her" (i.e., a man of a lower social status), his status improved and he now became her lord as well as master of all her property and wealth (Papp & Kirkland 74).

Directions: Draw or write what you have just heard on your sheet.

Following the Ceremony

- Marriage ceremonies required two witnesses. In more public ceremonies, the couple was sent off to bed by the wedding guests, and the marriage bed was blessed by the priest (Crispen).

- Consummation of the marriage was an important act in making the union official. This consummation was believed to be like God's coupling of the husband and wife's souls (Crispen).

- Men were considered the superior and all-powerful member of the couple, in both intellect and virtue. Women were expected to defer to their husband's wishes because the marital union was in keeping with the concept of divine order: God rules the universe, the king rules the country, and a husband rules his family (Griffin).

- A husband or wife could leave the marriage for only a few reasons: the partner was guilty of heresy or infidelity, the partner was seriously disfigured, the partner was legally still married to someone else, or the partner was guilty of wickedness or drunkenness ("Life in Elizabethan England").

Directions: Draw or write on your sheet what you have just heard. What symbols, words, and phrases work best to summarize this information?

Mini-Lesson 4: Masks, Masques, and Masquerades

Directions: Draw or write the key words or images from what I am about to explain.

Explanations: In act 1, Romeo and his friends attend a masquerade ball thrown by Juliet's father. To avoid detection, they wear masks. Masks were often made of leather and had grotesque, exaggerated features. Mercutio even talks about his disguise with its "beetle-brows"—heavy, pronounced eyebrows and/or forehead—and jokes that this ugly "visor" he places on his face is no worse than his own face. During Elizabethan times, dance parties were not the only occasions when people wore facades. The English, especially those involved in the king or queen's court, also participated in masques, a complex form of entertainment that involved disguises, acting, singing, music, and architecture. Usually the masque was offered in honor of an important person—Queen Elizabeth I, for example. Sometimes professional actors assumed the jobs; at other times, amateurs played the roles. According to Wikipedia ("Masque"), to stage a masque (also known as a pageant), people would organize a performance for a single night, planning the architecture and decorations of the room, developing the costumes, finding musicians, and possibly writing scripts. Because the masque was a huge production, combining so many different art forms all at once and requiring complex stage settings and costumes, it was usually never performed again. Even though Christianity was important during Shakespeare's time, many masques relied on classical stories—in other words, tales drawn from Greek and Roman writers, or from the old mythology. Shakespeare presents masques in *A Midsummer Night's Dream* and *The Tempest*. He uses a masked ball in *Romeo and Juliet*. In many plays, masks are important motifs, relating to the theme of identity.

Directions: What words or symbols will best represent the information just shared?

Explanations: Masks became associated with fun and wild parties beginning in Renaissance Italy, where Roman Catholics celebrated Carnival, a ten-day period before Lent during which citizens held pageants (masques), concerts, balls, and plays. Masks abounded, and people didn't just cover their faces: they also wore cloaks and capes to cover their bodies. Feeling historical? Don a famous face such as that of Cleopatra or Alexander the Great. Got money in your pocket? Invest in an elaborate mask that's gilded (decorated with precious metals) or one with a fantastical face or heavenly body (moon, sun).

Directions: Turn to a partner or form a triad and discuss what might happen when people are suddenly unrecognizable in terms of social status.

Explanations: Think about the nonstop craziness infecting the streets: everyone's anonymous, so anything goes. People with all this freedom consider their infinite options: Why not play a prank on someone of superior social status? Steal a kiss from a man or woman you don't know? Why not commit a crime? The crowds are thick and distractions—jugglers, magicians, mimes, and acrobats—are everywhere, so picking a pocket or pinching a rear is not hard to accomplish. Many people are drunk. Therefore the rules of society can be flouted (rebelled against), and hidden desires can be pursued.

Name_____ Period_____

Act 1 Reading Quiz

1. The Prince threatens which of the following to the warring Montagues and Capulets:

   a. Jail time for the next person who starts a brawl

   b. Death to those who ever disturb the peace again

   c. Fines and jail time for anyone who ever disturbs the peace

   d. Banishment (expulsion) of both families from Verona

2. Romeo is depressed because

   a. A woman he loved just ended a relationship with him because he has sworn to remain a virgin until marriage

   b. He just ended a relationship with a woman and now wants her back

   c. The woman he loves told him he is unattractive

   d. The woman he loves does not love him and swears she'll be a virgin till marriage

3. Lord Capulet's final response to Paris's proposal to marry Juliet is

   a. "Come to the party I'm throwing and see if you can win Juliet's heart"

   b. "Come to the party because there will be other women to see there"

   c. "Talk to me when she's older and ready for marriage"

   d. "Come back when you have a larger dowry to offer"

4. Benvolio's suggestion to remedy Romeo's depression is

   a. "Let's crash the Capulet party so you and your ex-girlfriend can work things out."

   b. "Let's crash the Capulet party since Lord Capulet has a beautiful daughter Juliet."

   c. "Let's crash the Capulet party so you can compare the woman you love to other beautiful women there and fall in love with someone else."

   d. "Let's spy on the Capulet party and get revenge by playing pranks on the guests."

5. Lady Capulet's discussion with Juliet and the Nurse concerns

   a. Whether Juliet is old enough at fourteen to be married

   b. Whether Juliet wants marriage and whether she can love Paris

   c. Whether Juliet is allowed to have men court her

   d. Whether the Nurse thinks Juliet is ready for romance

6. On the way to crashing the Capulet party, Romeo has a feeling that

   a. Fate might bring him an early death

   b. He will meet the woman of his dreams tonight

   c. His friends are too rowdy to get away with crashing the party

   d. His parents wouldn't approve of him crashing his enemies' party

7. At the Capulets', Romeo and Juliet speak in figurative language with images of

   a. Angels and cherubs

   b. Pilgrims and saints

   c. Roses and sunsets

   d. Dreams and wishes

8. Choose the only line that is not a metaphor from these quotations:

   a. "My life is my foe's debt."

   b. "Love is a smoke made with the fume of sighs."

   c. "You kiss by th' book."

   d. "If I profane with my unworthiest hand / This holy shrine"

9. Choose the simile from these examples:

   a. "O teach me how I should forget to think."

   b. "The all-seeing sun / Ne'er saw her match since the world first begun."

   c. "Why, he's a man of wax."

   d. "[I]t had upon it brow / A bump as big as a young cock'rel's stone."

10. Choose the oxymoron from these examples:

   a. "sick health"

   b. "transparent heretics"

   c. "rank poison"

   d. "choking gall."

Teaching Romeo and Juliet: *A Differentiated Approach* by Delia DeCourcy, Lyn Fairchild, and Robin Follet © 2007 NCTE.

3 Act 2: Lessons, Activities, and Handouts

Act 2, Scene 2

Lesson 2.a: On the Balcony of Love

Student Content and Skill Understandings

- Prepare to read and engage with a Shakespeare text. (AS)
- Use literary terms to articulate interpretations of narrative and character (AS) and themes. (OT/ADV)
- Recognize and use basic film terms in preparation for watching film versions of *Romeo and Juliet*. (AS)

Themes

- Love and marriage
- Identity
- Rebellion

Motifs

- Night/day
- Light/dark
- Sun/moon
- Time: haste v. slowness
- Masks

Materials

- 2.a.1: Shakescholar Close Reader: On the Balcony of Love A and B (assigned for homework the night before)
- 2.a.2: *Romeo and Juliet* on Film handout
- 2.a.3: Mini-Lesson 1: More 'n' More Motifs

Activities

STEP 1. OPTIONAL. WCA: I'm in the Mood for Love (5 minutes)

1. Use an anchoring activity such as a journal entry so that students can explore either of the following topics:

   a. NOV: What makes for a truly romantic moment. Is it roses and chocolates? Sweet nothings? Your best duds? A candlelit dinner? What constitutes a romantic gesture?

   b. OT/ADV: Which of the following motifs seem most romantic to you and why? Select at least one from this list and discuss the connotations of such words and how these motifs might appear in a romantic scene. Choose from night/day, light/dark, or sun/moon, time: haste v. slowness, or masks.

2. Consider teaching a mini-lesson on motifs to encourage close reading for patterns and trends that relate to greater themes. See handout 2.a.3.

STEP 2. TR Groups: Homework Review (25 minutes)

1. Put students in TR groups of three or four based on readiness.

2. Ask students to reread the balcony scene, using the already completed 2.a.1: On the Balcony of Love A and B handouts, pausing to confer about the answers to their CR questions and the themes evident in the scene. Ask TR questions from both CRs.

3. Circulate among the groups to check for understanding and assist as needed.

STEP 3. Key Elements of Film: A Mini-Lecture (20 minutes)

Review the *Romeo and Juliet* on Film handout, which defines the elements of a film's "cinematic texture." Explain that these elements are critical to our experience of a film version of a Shakespeare play, illustrating the director's interpretation of Shakespeare's script: (a) casting, (b) costumes, (c) sound effects and sound track, (d) camera angles, (e) blocking, (f) acting, and (g) line selection. Explain that Shakespeare's text is often cut and even rewritten. You can review the camera angle terms by asking a student to pose as a cameraperson and take the position from which the shots will be taken, asking students to sketch out the shots or angles on the board or in their notes, or asking them to use a lightweight picture frame to "frame" people in the room as if captured in a shot. Students can also share examples of famous shots or angles from films. For a fun introduction to the importance of sound effects, play the podcasts listed below from NPR's *Morning Edition* reports so that the creative work of Foley (sound effects) artists and costume designers will be clarified for students. Knowing more about these exciting careers will pique the interest of students and open a window to the behind-the-scenes efforts necessary to create a film. Such information might also help certain students choose interest-based skill strand assignments later, so consider recommending these Web links to individual students:

- "How Hollywood Makes Noise," 2-20-07. The creative work of Foley artists will be interesting to many students and open a window to the behind-the-scenes efforts necessary to create a film. Found at http://www.npr.org/templates/story/story.php?storyId=7400850.

- "Costume Designer Dips into Hollywood's Closet," 2-22-07. The creative work of costume designers. Found at http://www.npr.org/templates/story/story.php?storyId=7474294.

STEP 4. WCA: Prediction Options (5 minutes)

Ask students one or more of these questions:

1. What cinematic texture would you recommend for the balcony scene? Why?

2. How have themes of identity, rebellion, and dichotomy and paradox and the motif of masks manifested thus far in the balcony scene?

Epilogue: Suggested Homework

Assign other scenes in act 2 for independent reading, asking students to take notes using key words or symbols, or whatever note-taking system you recommend. Consider assigning cinematic skill strand activities (see the skill strand activities for acts 2–5 at the end of the chapter on page 188).

Notes on Differentiation

For step 1 of this lesson, consider allowing student choice even though the questions are TR. For step 3 of this lesson, consider a jigsaw teaching option. In MR groups, students review an assigned selection of film terms and prepare to teach them by developing oral explanations, visuals, and/or charade demonstrations. Then each student is reassigned to a new MR group and teaches his or her terms to group members, who also teach theirs.

Since there are two levels of TR close readers, encourage ADV students to pursue the challenge questions.

If you did not use the CRs for act 1, scene 4, then you will need to teach the Quotation Sandwich as a mini-lesson so that students who complete CR 2.a.1 B can complete the exercise. The Quotation Sandwich is an important mini-lesson for essay writing that will help students provide essential context and commentary for the evidence they use in an essay.

Shakescholar Close Reader 2.a.1: On the Balcony of Love A

Act 2, Scene 2, lines _____

Read act 2, scene 2, starting with Romeo's line, "But soft, what light through yonder window breaks," and ending with Juliet's line, "that I shall say good night till it be morrow." Answer the questions. As you read:

1. Use your Tips for Tackling the Language handout.
2. Refer to the reference notes in your play text.
3. Highlight the two most important words in each line. (Hint: look for important nouns and verbs.)
4. Draw a symbol next to every quotation to represent the most important feeling or action of the moment.
5. Answer these questions.

Questions:

1. Before you read, predict what will happen in this scene. Why did you make such a prediction?

   _____

   _____

ROMEO: The brightness of her cheek would shame those stars,

As daylight doth a lamp; her eyes in heaven

Would through the airy region stream so bright

That birds would sing and think it were not night.

See, how she leans her cheek upon her hand!

O, that I were a glove upon that hand,

That I might touch that cheek!

2. What kind of love is Romeo experiencing when he sees Juliet? Is it true romantic love or is it lust?

_____

_____

3. **CHALLENGE QUESTION:** What words in this passage have the same connotations (meaning, they all belong to the same "family" of words because they all have the same associations)? List these words below.

_____

_____

JULIET: O Romeo, Romeo! wherefore art thou Romeo?

Deny thy father and refuse thy name;

Or, if thou wilt not, be but sworn my love,

And I'll no longer be a Capulet.

4. Why does Juliet want Romeo to give up his name?

_____

_____

JULIET: O, be some other name!

What's in a name? that which we call a rose

By any other name would smell as sweet;

So Romeo would, were he not Romeo call'd,

Retain that dear perfection which he owes

Without that title. Romeo, doff thy name,

And for that name which is no part of thee

Take all myself.

5. What happens to a rose if we stop calling it a rose?

_____

_____

6. What does Juliet say will happen if Romeo is called by another name?

_____

_____

JULIET: If they do see thee, they will murder thee.

ROMEO: I have night's cloak to hide me from their sight;

   And but thou love me, let them find me here:

   My life were better ended by their hate,

   Than death prorogued, wanting of thy love.

7. Why would Juliet's people murder Romeo if they found him on her balcony?

_____

_____

8. How does Romeo feel about the possibility of being killed by the Capulets?

_____

_____

9. Why is Juliet nervous when she begins her speech that starts "Dost thou love me?"

_____

_____

10. What does Juliet mean when she says, "Do not swear at all; / Or, if thou wilt, swear by thy gracious self, / Which is the god of my idolatry, / And I'll believe thee?"

_____

_____

11. Before he goes, Romeo says, "O, wilt thou leave me so unsatisfied?" Juliet responds with, "What satisfaction

canst thou have to-night?" What does Romeo want before he goes?

_____

_____

JULIET: Three words, dear Romeo, and good night
indeed.

If that thy bent of love be honourable,

Thy purpose marriage, send me word
to-morrow,

By one that I'll procure to come to thee,

Where and what time thou wilt perform the rite;

And all my fortunes at thy foot I'll lay

And follow thee my lord throughout the world.

12. Read the lines above and explain what the plan is if
Romeo's love is true and his intentions are real.

_____

_____

13. Juliet forgets why she called Romeo back. List some reasons why a girlfriend might call her boyfriend back after they have parted.

_____

_____

JULIET: 'Tis almost morning; I would have thee gone:

And yet no further than a wanton's bird;

Who lets it hop a little from her hand,

Like a poor prisoner in his twisted gyves,

And with a silk thread plucks it back again,

So loving-jealous of his liberty.

14. Juliet imagines Romeo as a bird and herself as owner of this bird. What words seem most important in this **simile**? Why? What do we learn about how she feels about Romeo?

_____

_____

CHALLENGE: Did you see the **motif** of time: **haste** v. slowness anywhere in this scene? Where? Copy down the quotations.

SUPER CHALLENGE: Write an explanation that comments on whether the references to time are positive or negative and whether they are associated with any particular characters.

Glossary:
haste: quickness, swiftness, speed; *haste* can have the connotation of unnecessary speed or urgency
motif: a repeated symbol in a literary work that is often a sensory, physical image and vehicle of concepts in the literary work. Motifs represent patterns or trends that lead to theme.
simile: a comparison of two things using *like* or *as*

Shakescholar Close Reader 2.a.1: On the Balcony of Love B

Act 2, Scene 2

Read act 2, scene 2 in its entirety. As you read, do the following:

1. Keep a dialectical journal for this scene by recording quotations that are significant instances of the following themes and motifs (at least one of each):

   Themes: Identity, love and marriage: love at first sight or true romantic love, rebellion

   Motifs: night/day, light/dark, or sun/moon, time: haste v. slowness, masks

2. Highlight the four to ten lines that you believe are the most significant to the scene and write an explanation—a Quotation Sandwich—justifying why you chose these.

Answer the following questions on a separate sheet of paper:

1. Closely read Romeo's first nine lines. Explain why he compares Juliet to the sun and wants her to "kill the envious moon." What is the meaning of this metaphor? (Hint: think about the **denotations** of words like *sun* and *moon* as well as their connotations—the associations, images, and emotions we attach to such words.)

2. Explain why Juliet wants Romeo to cast off his name. As you write your explanation, comment on how this request relates to a key theme in this play.

3. Beginning at line 85, Juliet expresses some anxiety. Why? What are the sources of this worry?

4. How would you **characterize** the love expressed in this scene? What kind of love is it? Quote lines from both characters to support your point.

5. Consider all the entrances and exits in the scene. Why would Shakespeare include so many false endings to the scene? What does Shakespeare's choice tell the reader about the characters and their situation?

6. **CHALLENGE QUESTION:** Track the following motifs in this scene: interior/exterior spaces, looking/sight, and nature. Which motif best represents the love between Romeo and Juliet? Why?

7. CHALLENGE QUESTION:

a. How is this scene between the lovers both romantic and dangerous? Find a quotation for each quality present. Is the romance **enhanced** by the presence of danger, or would it be more romantic not to be in danger?

b. Do the words that Romeo and Juliet use foreshadow good or bad events to come? Track the use of positive versus negative words in the scene (hint: look at motifs and key nouns and verbs) and justify your answer with two reasons: (i) the number of positive versus negative words and (ii) the **connotations** of such words—what they might predict.

c. Is there any **subtext** not expressed by Romeo and Juliet in this scene, or do they expose all the deepest feelings of their hearts? What do you learn about Romeo's and Juliet's identities from this scene?

Glossary:
characterize: to describe the qualities
connotations: associations, implications, and impressions that come to mind when a word is said; not the exact definition, but the impression a word gives.
denotation: literal or dictionary definition
enhanced: made greater, bigger, better
subtext: hidden emotions and thoughts

Teaching Romeo and Juliet: *A Differentiated Approach* by Delia DeCourcy, Lyn Fairchild, and Robin Follet © 2007 NCTE.

Handout 2.a.2: *Romeo and Juliet* on Film

Choices toward the Cinematic Texture

Casting: decisions about who will play the various roles in the film.

Costume design: the actors' wardrobe and accessories, determined by the setting, time period, and mood of the film or a particular scene.

Sound track: the music selected to play during scenes in the film, adding to the emotional sense.

Cinematic shots/camera angles: the movement in the shot, the length of the shot, and the angle of the screen image. A *cut* is a shift between two different camera shots.

Camera Work: Movement, Angle, and Length

Movement: (1) a series of cuts that go from one shot to the next or (2) moving the camera with the action—a slower option because the amount of visual information on the screen decreases in relation to time, especially when compared to a series of quick cuts. Some methods of camera movement include (a) **zoom lens shot:** a shot that moves the viewer in or out of a scene quickly without the camera having to move while filming, often giving a distorted sense of the people or objects on screen; (b) **aerial shots:** taken from a helicopter, often used as "establishing shots" at the film's beginning, allowing the camera to move fluidly about the landscape; (c) **handheld shots:** the camera is attached with a harness to the camera operator, allowing the operator to move in and out of shots speedily; provides a bumpy visual experience for the viewer and thus the impression of realism (versus a dolly shot); (d) **tilts:** vertical camera movement through the scene; (e) **pans:** horizontal camera movement through the scene.

Angle: the placement of the camera in relation to the person or object being photographed. The angle at which the person or object is recorded provides the audience hints about the importance or relevance of what shows up on screen.

Oblique/canted angle: tilted, nonhorizontal angle used in point of view shots to allow the viewer to closely experience the fear, unsteadiness, or unease of a character.

Eye level: angle where the viewer observes the scene as if in the setting at eye level with the actors.

Low angle: angle low to the ground and tilted up so the object or actor in the frame appears larger than it or he or she is and may appear quite intimidating.

High angle: a version of the bird's-eye view that is less severe because the camera is not as elevated.

Bird's-eye view: angle where the viewer looks straight down on the scene from overhead. Objects can be made unrecognizable or people can be made to seem small and insignificant.

Length of shot (framing of the shot): the expanse of the shot, determined by what people, objects, and landscape appear in the camera's frame.

Close-up shot: a shot that focuses the viewer's eye on a face, an object, or a landscape detail, magnifying it across the screen, with the goal to express importance of whatever is in the frame. With a character, the shot suggests that we are entering the mind of the character.

Point of view shot: a shot from the point of view of a character, so the viewer experiences the action from the perspective of interacting with one or more of the other characters.

Over-the-shoulder shot: a type of medium shot where the camera looks over the shoulder of one character during a conversation so that viewers focus on one character at a time.

Medium shot: a shot that shows the interaction between characters by framing them from chest up. Often used for dialogue scenes, the shot normally contains two to three people.

Long shot: a shot showing the action and characters in life size with their full bodies on screen.

Extreme long shot: an "establishing shot" for the film, letting viewers know where the action occurs; an exterior shot from far away (see **bird's-eye view**).

(Definitions have been paraphrased from the following sources: "Describing Shots," "Directing," and "Glossary of Film Terms.")

Teaching Romeo and Juliet: *A Differentiated Approach* by Delia DeCourcy, Lyn Fairchild, and Robin Follet © 2007 NCTE.

Handout 2.a.3: Mini-Lesson 1: More 'n' More Motifs

Directions: Draw or write the key words or images from what I am about to explain.

Explanations: In act 1 we discussed masks and how that image appeared in the last scenes of the play. Masks in Romeo and Juliet are a literary device called a motif, which is a repeated symbol in a literary work that is often a sensory, physical image. Motifs represent patterns or trends that lead to theme. A theme is a "universal truth." For example, love is a theme, an idea that people understand and believe in and can make statements about, but love is not a motif. The sun and moon are motifs but not themes. The sun and moon might represent the themes of beauty or change. The rose you give someone on Valentine's day is a motif of love.

Directions: What key words did you hear in this definition? (Students should note words such as *repeated, symbol, sensory,* and *vehicle.*)

Explanation: Here are some motifs you have already seen in act 1:

      a. night/day, light/dark, or sun/moon

      b. time: haste v. slowness

      c. masks

Directions: Turn to a partner and flip through the text of act 1 to search for quotations that refer to the motifs of night/day, light/dark, or sun/moon.

Explanation: (direct students to find these quotations if they cannot find references):

Night/day, light/dark, sun/moon quotations:

      a. "Away from night steals home my heavy son, . . .
         Locks fair daylight out,
         And makes himself an artificial night" (Lord Montague, 1.1)

      b. "Compare her face with some that I shall show,
         And I will make thee think thy swan a crow." (Benvolio, 1.1)

      c. "One fairer than my love! The all-seeing sun
         Ne'er saw her match since the world begun." (Romeo, 1.2)

   d. "O she doth teach the torches to burn bright!
      It seems she hangs upon the cheek of night
      As a rich jewel in an Ethiop's ear . . ." (Romeo, 1.5)

Directions: Discuss these questions with a partner and report back to the class:

   a. What associations do we make with day versus night, light versus dark, white versus black, and the sun versus the moon? Are these associations positive or negative?

   b. What idiomatic expressions and figurative language express the human attitude toward these elements?

Directions: Turn to a partner and together flip through the text of act 1 (or any other act if you have read ahead). Choose one of the following challenges:

   1. NOV/OT: Look for the motif of *time: haste v. slowness* and find quotations. Then discuss what connotations such words have and whether these associations are positive or negative. What idiomatic expressions and figurative language express cultural attitudes toward time, haste, and slowness? (Think of expressions your family or friends have about time.)

   2. ADV: Look for new motifs we have not yet discussed. Look for important nouns, verbs, adjectives, and adverbs that create an image in your head. Discuss whether these images might reveal motifs, repeated images that could relate to a theme. Remember that motifs represent patterns or trends that lead to theme, which is a "universal truth." So you should look especially for concrete nouns, not abstract nouns, as you read.

Explanation:

   1. NOV/OT: Share some of your quotations for the motif of time: haste v. slowness and discuss the connotations and idiomatic cultural expressions relating to time.

   2. ADV: Share some of your motif findings. Do your suggested motifs meet the Motif Test?

      ▪ You can picture an image when you hear or read the word.

      ▪ The image is repeated more than once in a scene or

act, and the words used to describe these images have similar connotations.

- The words for the motif are not abstract but concrete.

Directions: As you continue to read the play, look for these motifs (mention if ADV students have not already noted some of these):

- Interior/exterior spaces
- Looking/sight
- Nature

Lesson 2.b: Zeffirelli and Luhrmann on Shakespeare

Student Content and Skill Understandings

- Define and use, both in written work and discussion, the basic language of film. (AS)
- Identify and explain how camera angles and lighting influence the viewer's understanding and interpretation of the film. (AS)
- Explain how film adaptations of Shakespeare's plays function as a visual form of literary criticism, focusing particularly on what elements of the film remain faithful to the written text and what is cut and/or rearranged within the adaptation. (OT/ADV)

Themes

- Love and marriage
- Identity
- Rebellion

Motifs

- Time: haste v. slowness

Materials

- *Romeo and Juliet* film versions by Franco Zeffirelli and Baz Luhrmann
- 2.b.1: *Romeo and Juliet* Shakescholar Film Analysis Close Reader
- 2.b.2: Film Review Assignments A, B, and C

Activities

STEP 1. WCA: Film Study (35 minutes)

1. Explain to students that now that they have read the balcony scene and reviewed film terms, they are prepared to watch two film versions and compare the choices of each filmmaker in interpreting Shakespeare's text. Preview the questions you will be discussing as a class (see step 2).

2. Give students their 2.b.1 Film Analysis CRs to complete while viewing the films; review your expectations of how to complete the CR so students know what to look for as they watch the films.

3. View the Franco Zeffirelli film version of the balcony scene first. It is truer to the original text (14 minutes long). Suggestion: pause halfway through for students to fill in their CRs. Give students a few minutes to fill in their chart following the Zeffirelli clip as needed.

4. View the Baz Luhrmann version of the balcony scene (9 minutes). Suggestion: pause halfway through for students to fill in their CRs.

STEP 2. WCA: Film Discussion (10 minutes)

1. Lead a class discussion in which students share their observations about the directorial choices, camera angles, and overall visual effectiveness of each film. Begin by discussing the ideas students have recorded on their CRs. Follow-up questions might include:

   - NOV/OT: What is similar about the two interpretations' casting, sound track/sound effects, and cinematic shots/camera angles?

   - NOV/OT: How does the pace of the two films compare? Name a moment from each film that best captures the pace of each.

   - NOV: How does Luhrmann modernize his version? Name objects that could not have existed in Shakespeare's time.

   - OT/ADV: Does this modernization add to or distract us from the text?

   - ADV: How does the adaptation of this play into a film alter it? What are the differences in the way we experience the film versions versus how we could experience a stage adaptation? What are the challenges, benefits, and drawbacks of stage performance versus a cinematic version?

STEP 3. WCA: Discussion (5 minutes)

1. ADV: Ask students to name the themes that Luhrmann and/or Zeffirelli portrayed most strongly

in their films, with references to specific elements of cinematic texture as proof.

2. Tell students that for homework they will write a film review, considering in more depth the choices these directors made. Hand out 2.b.2: Film Review Assignments A, B, and C.

Epilogue: Suggested Homework

Ask students to write a film review based their viewing experience today. Allow students to select A, B, or C according to their own sense of their readiness level.

Notes on Differentiation

1. For step 1.3, students can work in MR partners or alone for both analyses. For classes of lower readiness level, consider MR partners rather than independent work.

2. For step 2, you can replace WCA discussion with TR groπ»s and then follow up with a WCA discussion.

3. ADV questions on the CRs include capturing the scene's tone or mood, analysis that requires students to synthesize elements of cinematic texture under one generalization or theme. The camera angles question will appeal to students with ADV visual-spatial skills.

4. If you decide to develop CRs for other scenes that you would like students to read closely, consider asking them to analyze Friar Laurence's soliloquy on herbs, virtue, and vice (scene 3) and Juliet's soliloquy on her love and "old folks" (scene 5).

5. Consider opening and closing class with journals and/ or theme discussions. Here are some possible options:

   a. Love and Marriage

      i. NOV: What kinds of love do the two lovers express in the balcony scene? OT/ADV: How do the different types of love play into their decision at the scene's end?

      ii. NOV: Their decision is to marry. What is your opinion of this plan to marry?

b. Identity

    i. NOV/OT: How do Romeo's and Juliet's family identities affect their behavior and decisions in this act? Would the act have turned out differently if they had not been from feuding families? How? Why?

c. Rebellion

    i. ADV: Teenagers often feel they have limited power while living in their parents' house and having to follow their parents' rules. Explain how the budding relationship and possible marriage between Romeo and Juliet is a form of rebellion. Do you think these characters are aware of their actions as a form of rebellion? What are they rebelling against, if anything?

    ii. OT: The garden is a place where Romeo can mask himself so that Capulets won't find him and possibly murder him. Are there any other elements of the scenery that mask the lovers or unmask them?

Handout 2.b.1: *Romeo and Juliet* Shakescholar Film Analysis Close Reader

Act 2, Scene 2

Film Element	Zeffirelli Version	Similarities	Luhrmann Version
Setting Time period: What are the indicators? Location of scene?			
Costumes Describe overall design with adjectives. Name one representative character and his or her costume details.			
Camera Angles Length, angle, vantage point, camera movement. When do we see a lot of movement? When is the screen more still? List at least three angles that strike you as important to the scene: • What type are they? • What emotions and perspective do they convey?	1. 2. 3. 4. 5. 6.	Any similar angles for particular parts of Shakespeare's text?	1. 2. 3. 4. 5. 6.

Blocking Actors' movement in relation to one another and the space Note significant blocking choices during scene. What actions show character identity? What actions mark important plot points? When is there a lot of character move-ment versus stillness?	1. 2. 3.	Similarities in Romeo's blocking in these films?	1. 2. 3.
Acting Choices/ Direction Actors interpret their lines and character reactions through choices in emotional level, facial expression, vocal inflection and volume, and gesture. Note significant choices and accom-panying lines. What choices show character identity?	Romeo Juliet	How are the Romeos similar? How are the Juliets similar?	Romeo Juliet

Lines Cut from Original Text	What's missing?	What would you have cut from the scene?	What's missing?
Adjectives to describe the tone/ mood of scene			

HANDOUT 2.b.2: Film Review Assignment

Film Review Assignment A

Choose your favorite balcony scene to review. You are a film critic writing for a major magazine and the votes are in: _____'s version of the balcony scene is the best!

1. Write three body paragraphs in which you explain the three most effective cinematic elements of the film and why these were effective. Use the film chart to choose among these elements: setting, costumes, blocking, acting choices, or camera angles.

2. Write a paragraph arguing in support of each cinematic element. Begin each paragraph with "The element of _____ is most effective because _____."

3. Prove your argument in each paragraph for "most effective" by providing *specific* details from the film to support your opinion. If you need to mention the other film version that made a less effective choice, do so to show how the film you chose was better.

4. Write your thesis paragraph last. Introduce the essay, listing the three most effective cinematic elements and why they were so important to this balcony scene's success. Remember to keep this paragraph brief and to use general words, not specific examples, to summarize your reasons.

Film Review Assignment B

1. Write a film review in which you compare and contrast three cinematic elements used in each film's balcony scene.

2. Write three body paragraphs, one per cinematic element. The topic sentence of each body paragraph should mention both films and your decision about the effectiveness of the use of the element in each.

3. Prove your argument for effectiveness or ineffectiveness by providing at least two *specific* examples, one from each film, to support your opinion.

4. Write your thesis paragraph last. Remember to keep this paragraph brief and to use general words, not specific

examples, to summarize which elements were effectively or ineffectively used and the reasons why.

Film Review Assignment C

Option 1

1. Write a review that analyzes the cinematic texture of one or both films' balcony scenes. Identify the thematic, emotional mood that the cinematic texture evokes and which cinematic elements contribute to this texture.

2. Write at least three body paragraphs that are coherent and unified around one or two cinematic elements. Each paragraph's topic sentence needs to name the cinematic element(s) and the ways the director's or directors' use of it contributes to the thematic, emotional mood of the film.

3. Provide at least three specific examples to prove how the thematic, emotional mood is created by a particular element. If you discuss more than one cinematic element in a paragraph, be sure to cite at least two examples per element.

4. Write your thesis paragraph last. Remember to keep this paragraph brief and to use general words, not specific examples, to summarize the thematic and emotional mood of the cinematic texture, as well as which elements were used to create it.

Option 2

Which version is truer to Shakespeare's text? Does remaining truer to the text translate to a more effective cinematic interpretation of *Romeo and Juliet*? Why or why not? How does cutting the text affect the balcony scene? Argue for the effectiveness of one film version or the other in relation to textual accuracy, using the paragraphing format described above.

Teaching Romeo and Juliet: *A Differentiated Approach* by Delia DeCourcy, Lyn Fairchild, and Robin Follet © 2007 NCTE.

Skill Strands

Drama

1. Soliloquy Memorization: Memorize a soliloquy from any act and present it with attention to iambic pentameter, correct pronunciation, articulation, pacing, and volume. Seek coaching from a drama professional.

2. Director's Promptbook: Create a director's promptbook for any scene from act 2–5.

3. Setting Adaptation: Rewrite a scene from any act by setting it in your hometown or city. Adapt the language and actions of the characters to the cultural traits and themes of our historical era, as well as your community's culture, and revise the script accordingly.

4. Performance: Present any scene from the play with conscious choices about acting/blocking, costumes, scenery, music, and other features that demonstrate the larger theme(s). Work cooperatively in a small group, dividing tasks of directing, acting, and design.

5. Motif Tracking: Create a storyboard of motif ideas for a theater director, advising him or her on how to use symbolic objects and scenery to stage the play. Motifs can appear in the scenery, props, and/or costumes.

6. Shakespeare, Inc. Project: Complete the Shakespeare, Inc. project (handout on pages 194–96).

Cinema

1. Oh Nurse, Oh Nurse: The Nurse plays a critical role in act 2. She arranges the marriage of Romeo and Juliet, making this a good place to study both Zeffirelli's and Luhrmann's casting choices for the Nurse and the actresses' portrayal of this character. After watching act 2 of both films, write an essay in which you compare the following: (1) the "type" of actress cast as the Nurse for the 1996 version (Miriam Margolyes) and the 1968 version (Pat Heywood); (2) the actresses' depiction of the

Nurse with regard to: (a) her physical presence (appearance and way of moving through the space); (b) her relationship with Juliet; (c) her relationship with Lady Capulet; (d) her interaction with the Montague boys when she meets Romeo to hear his intentions; (e) her delivery of the Shakespearean text; (f) your interpretation of how the depiction of the Nurse in each film affects the rest of the film.

2. Motif Tracking: Create a storyboard of motif ideas for a theater director, advising him or her on how to use symbolic objects and scenery to film the play. Motifs can appear in the scenery, props, and/or costumes.

3. Create a poster or project board on which you track significant motifs or symbols in the Baz Luhrmann version of *Romeo and Juliet*. Provide an image to represent each motif or symbol, explain its significance in the film, and list the scenes in which it is used and to what effect. Possible motifs and symbols include:

   - Water
   - Fire
   - Religion: angels, demons, crosses, and so forth
   - Stages/theater
   - Masks/costumes

Creative Writing

Missed Connections

Have you ever seen the Missed Connections section of the personals in a newspaper? People who met briefly or merely locked eyes at a stoplight and want to reconnect put an ad in Missed Connections hoping to find that person who they think might be their soul mate.

Pretend that Romeo does not know how to get to Juliet's balcony and so is not able to **profess** his interest in her. Instead, he must put an ad in the Missed Connections section of the *Verona Times*. Write his ad in which you **convey** the **essence** of what he says to Juliet in the balcony scene in fifty words or less. You must also make it clear to Juliet, should she happen to read the ad, whom the **epistle** is from without giving away the secret love to all other readers.

Pretend that Juliet was not out on her balcony following the Capulet ball to hear all the lovely compliments of her sweet Romeo. Instead, she must put an ad in the Missed Connections section of the *Verona Times*. Write her ad in which you convey the essence of what she says to Romeo in the balcony scene in fifty words or less. You must also make it clear to Romeo, should he happen to read the ad, whom the epistle is from without giving away the secret love to all other readers.

Glossary:
convey: show, demonstrate
essence: main idea, point
epistle: letter, message
profess: declare, admit

Socratic Discussion, Act 2

Love and Marriage: **Play-Related Questions**

- What indications do we have that Romeo and Juliet are experiencing lust?
- What indications do we have that they are experiencing love? Which feeling is stronger?

Love and Marriage: **Relevance Questions**

- Is love at first sight possible, or is it just physical attraction at work?
- What social barriers do people today face in their love lives?

Rebellion: **Play-Related Questions**

- The Nurse and the Friar both engage in forms of rebellion in this act. What kind of rebellion do they embrace? What is their motivation for breaking the social order?
- Think about Mercutio's behavior with Romeo and Benvolio in acts 1 and 2. In what ways is he the rebellious leader? If there is a **continuum** of rebellion (1 being a conformist, **passive**, nonrebellious personality, and 10 being an anti-establishment, active, and rebellious personality), what ratings would you give Mercutio, Benvolio, and Romeo? Why?

Rebellion: Relevance Questions

- How and why do teenagers use romantic relationships to rebel against their parents?
- Do people tend to be more rebellious when they are with peers than when they're alone? In what ways do friendships encourage or discourage rebellion?

Dichotomy and Paradox: Play-Related Questions

- Consider Friar Laurence's soliloquy as an **explicit** statement of this key theme in the play. Where and how does the double-sided nature of many elements in the play present itself, when "virtue itself turns vice"? Consider some of the following oppositions: public/private, love/hate, comedy/tragedy, **intemperance/temperance**, youth/old age.
- Why does Shakespeare illustrate such **paradoxes**? How similar are these supposed opposites and what overall function do they have in the play?

Dichotomy and Paradox: Relevance Questions

- How can someone or something exhibit opposite characteristics? For example, how can you both love and hate someone? How can something be both a lifesaver and a deathtrap?

Identity: Play-Related Questions

- How do love and hate define the identities of the play's various characters, especially Romeo, Tybalt, Mercutio, and Juliet?

Glossary:
continuum: a sequence of values, with opposites at either end
explicit: completely revealed, openly stated
intemperance: reckless, lacking self-control
paradoxes: opposites coexisting
passive: submissive, not dominant, acted upon
temperance: controlled, self-regulating

Identity: **Relevance Questions**

- How do hate and love define our identities? Does society expect us to hold certain kinds of hates and loves? Do we personally expect it of ourselves?
- How much does our identity rely on others? In what ways? How are we defined by the existence of "the other"—our seeming opposite? Do opposites truly attract?

Time: Haste v. Slowness: **Play-Related Questions**

- How aware of the quickness of their love are Romeo and Juliet?

Time: Haste v. Slowness: **Relevance Questions**

- Is it better to love passionately? Or to love moderately? Why? How does love or any intense emotion affect a sense of time for you?
- Is love truer if it happens quickly? Why or why not?

Motifs: **Play-Related Questions**

- *Interior and exterior spaces*: How do the separations in the play—the walls between public and private space—mirror the emotional separations the characters experience?
- *Night and day, light and dark*: What imagery using night, day, light, and dark does Romeo use to describe Rosaline? How does he describe Juliet? What are the differences in these images? What occurs at night during the play? What is brought into the light of day? What is interesting about Shakespeare's choices to set the action in these times of day?
- *Looking and sight*: Why does Friar Laurence say that young men's love lies in their eyes, rather than in their hearts?
- *Masks*: How does Romeo mask or conceal himself in this act with both Juliet and Mercutio? How might his choice be significant?

Motifs: **Relevance Questions**

- *Interior and exterior spaces*: How do we separate the parts of our lives and identities using interior and exterior spaces?

- *Night and day, light and dark*: What associations do we make with the sun? The moon?

- *Looking and sight*: Do we judge most with sight? Or do we use other means of judging?

- *Masks*: How do masks provide a sense of security? Does falling in love tend to intensify the masking of identity or decrease it?

Shakespeare, Inc.: An Experiment in Theater and Finance

Shakespeare, Inc. needs a costume designer, stage designer, writer/director, or sound designer to make a new stage or film version of *Romeo and Juliet*. The board of directors is eager to hear your presentation, and if you are successful, you just might earn yourself $20,000—or more!

Form a company devoted to one of these roles (i.e., a costume-making company, a stage sets company, etc.). Develop a product based on your role. A costume designer must plan and draw costumes for *at least* three characters from the play. A stage designer must develop three possible proposals for set design. A writer/director must plan and present a partial scene that consists of 50 to 100 lines, or she or he must write three additional monologues. A sound designer must create a CD that uses different pieces of music and at least one sound effect for three different scenes. Produce high-quality products if you want the financial support.

Shakespeare Inc.'s Board and Its Director

Although the teacher, as director of the board, is ultimately responsible for the grading of the product, the board does have a choice about which project(s) it will fund. Toward that end, Shakespeare, Inc. has a $60,000 budget. Each project costs $20,000 to fund completely. Will the board fund your proposal completely? Will it give you partial funding? Only the board (i.e., your peers) can decide. Also contributing to your chances at financial support is your observed work as a team or as a solo artist. If you work as a team, all must contribute **diligently**. If you work alone, stay focused. Even one reminder to stay on task will result in a loss of points. We hire no slackers at Shakespeare, Inc. Discussions and debates will follow the presentations, and all the information available will be used.

To gain the Board's **approbation** (and to **maximize** your grade stock), your presentation proposal must include these three ingredients:

- *Performance*: An excerpt of your high-quality, thoughtfully constructed product, using whatever visual, sound, or **kinesthetic** effects to best present the scene (for example, a costume designer might present a fashion show or an array of sketches; a stage designer might present models or sketches; a writer/director might present a performed scene; a sound designer might present a cinematic or live acting montage, freeze-frame style, with new sound track included). Time limit: 5 minutes

- *Written **Justification***: An essay, including quotations from the play and explanations (three-paragraph minimum, five-paragraph maximum), to justify why these costumes/sets/lines or monologues/songs were chosen and/or created and presented this way. Each company member is responsible for writing one body paragraph justifying the company's choice. The director of the board will review this portion. Word limit: 1,250 words

- *Sales Pitch*: A brief speech that begins with an introduction explaining who your company is, why you are presenting, and why you deserve the grant money; a body of arguments presenting three distinct points that show how your ideas will help the play *Romeo and Juliet*; and a conclusion that reviews your main three points. The essay will serve as your notes for your presentation. Time limit: 5 minutes

Project Criteria	Incomplete	Competent	Excellent
Presentation (Sales Pitch): 1. Introduction (who you are, why you are here, and why your company deserves the grant) 2. Body (points effectively stated, each paragraph devoted to a clear and coherent explanation of one aspect of the presentation) 3. Conclusion (complete summary) 4. Polish and style (effective sales pitch)			
Product: 1. Creativity (uniqueness) of ideas 2. Quality (effort, thoroughness, polish)			
Essay: 1. Organization and **coherence** 2. Substantive evidence justifying each choice 3. **Rhetoric, diction**, voice toward a **compelling** argument			
Group Work or Solo Effort Work **ethic**, dedication, focus, drive			

Glossary:
approbation: approval
coherence: unity
compelling: powerful, causing respect and admiration, engaging
diction: word choice
diligently: persistently, painstakingly, in a manner that shows commitment
ethic: value, principle
justification: reasoning, explanation
kinesthetic: relating to use of the body (movement, dance, etc.)
maximize: to increase to the greatest degree
rhetoric: art and use of persuasive language
stock: supply, capital, as in financial investment

Teaching Romeo and Juliet: *A Differentiated Approach* by Delia DeCourcy, Lyn Fairchild, and Robin Follet © 2007 NCTE.

Name_____ Period_____

Act 2 Reading Quiz

1. When Romeo and Juliet swear love, they acknowledge their main challenge is:

    a. Their names and the feud (fight) between their families

    b. The Nurse's dislike of Juliet's suitors who don't first get her approval

    c. The fact that Romeo strangely believes Juliet's eyes are stars

    d. The curfew that Juliet's parents strictly enforce

2. "What's in a name? That which we call a rose / By any other word would smell as sweet." Juliet's quotation from the balcony scene means:

    a. Roses smell great. That is why they are named roses.

    b. No matter what we call a rose, it still smells wonderful. The name does not change the nature of the object.

    c. Names are like roses. Both smell good and describe the object they name.

    d. Juliet has a friend named Rose who she thinks is a very sweet person.

3. During the balcony scene, the two young lovers profess their true love and decide to

    a. Run away together to Mantua to escape the feud and their families' judgment

    b. Decide tomorrow where and when their marriage will occur

    c. Have a midnight snack together on Juliet's balcony before the guards chase Romeo away

    d. Go to the Montague ball together the following week

4. Which character interrupts Romeo and Juliet's conversation on the balcony but fortunately doesn't see Romeo?

    a. Lord Capulet

    b. Mercutio

c. Lady Capulet

d. The Nurse

5. Friar Laurence's declaration that "Virtue itself turns vice, being misapplied, / And vice sometimes by action dignified" is an example of which theme?

a. Dichotomy and paradox

b. Identity

c. Rebellion

d. Love and marriage

6. In act 2, scene 3, Friar Laurence agrees to help Romeo pursue his love for Juliet because

a. He thinks she is a better match for Romeo than Rosaline.

b. He just wants Romeo to settle down and get married.

c. He thinks their love might end the feud between their two families.

d. He is convinced that Romeo truly loves Juliet and wants them to be together.

7. When Benvolio, Mercutio, and Romeo run into the Nurse in the square and tease, badger, and harass her, the Nurse

a. Immediately goes home to Juliet and reports this bad behavior

b. Engages in their wordplay and naughty joking with good humor, though she seems a bit agitated (nervous and uncomfortable)

c. Sends her servant after the three young men, using her umbrella as a weapon

d. Slaps each of the young men hard on the face and calls them "rogues"

8. When the Nurse returns from her meeting with Romeo, she

a. Immediately tells Juliet the news of the plans for her upcoming wedding

b. Meets with Lord and Lady Capulet to discuss the distressing situation their daughter has gotten herself into

c. Demands that Juliet pay her for her services as messenger

d. Makes Juliet beg for the news by ignoring her questions and complaining that her head and back ache

9. Romeo and Juliet meet in the following place to exchange their wedding vows:

a. Juliet's balcony

b. Verona's city square

c. Friar Laurence's cell

d. The Montague home

Teaching Romeo and Juliet: *A Differentiated Approach* by Delia DeCourcy, Lyn Fairchild, and Robin Follet © 2007 NCTE.

4 Act 3: Lessons, Activities, and Handouts

Act 3, Scene 1

Lesson 3.a: Mercurial Mercutio

Student Content and Skill Understandings

- Prepare to read and engage with a Shakespeare text. (AS)
- Summarize plot. (AS)
- Identify and explicate a character's traits using the character's actions, speech, appearance, and reactions from other characters. (AS)

Themes

- Rebellion
- Love
- Identity

Materials and Handouts

- 3.a.1: Mercurial Mercutio handout
- Props and symbolic representations of Verona's town square (students can bring in simple props such as sheets, boxes, blocks, and other items to form scenery such as a fountain, different levels such as steps to the Prince's quarters, symbols of Capulet and Montague dominance, or any other stage sets they might deem necessary)

Activities

STEP 1. WCA: Mini-Lesson or Student Lecture (10 minutes)

1. Provide a brief summary of act 3.
2. Ask students to make some initial suggestions based on this summary about the body positions, gestures, and facial expressions of actors (acting), as well as the blocking (movement of actors and props in relation

to one another and use of stage space), that will bring this summary to life. What expression should Tybalt wear? What gestures should Mercutio make? How should actors confront one another?

STEP 2. WCA: Scenelet Demonstration (30 minutes)

1. Ask for four students to volunteer as actors in training, willing to take direction. Pass out handout 3.a.1: Mercurial Mercutio to these students and ask them to practice elsewhere.

2. Ask three to five students to create a stage in the room suitable to the summarized action. Ask these students how they will create a space that best represents Verona's central gathering spot using the props they have been handed. They should use the past events of the play, particularly act 1's opening scene, to justify their choices for stage design.

3. Ask all other students to form pairs or triads and "take a number" to play director. You might have 15–20 student director pairs. Ask these students to discuss the following question as they review the play text, beginning with Benvolio's line "By my head . . ." and ending with Mercutio's line, "I will not budge . . .": How should we direct this scene to create a feeling of intensity, danger, and impending tragedy? The pairs should make notes on the handout to prepare to advise the actors.

4. Ask the actors to present the partial scene to the class as directed by the handout; meanwhile, the student director pairs should be making suggestions in their notes regarding acting and blocking.

5. Ask the actors to perform again and this time be directed by the class. As the teacher holds up numbers, the designated student directing pair calls "Freeze!" and takes its turn suggesting acting or blocking tips. The teacher calls "Rerun!" to have the actors present revisions. The teacher can also call "Text check!" at random times so that directorial pairs or actors must justify how the play's text calls for the choices they have recommended.

6. Lead a discussion with an ADV question: how has Shakespeare's text inspired multiple possibilities for performance?

Epilogue: Suggested Homework

As students read scenes for homework, ask them to make director's notes.

Notes on Differentiation

1. For step 1 of this lesson, consider using a compacting student to help provide an overview of act 3 necessary for the next set of lessons.

2. This activity and those that follow will help students consider and experience multiple interpretations of the same snippets of act 3, scene 1. Through shared experimentation, they will come to a greater understanding of the dramatic possibilities contained in the play. Not only do you address different learning styles in this practice performance, but you also allow students creative play. Very simple props challenge student creativity, as does the structure of "handing" them the themes of intensity, danger, and impending tragedy. Multiple ways of showing these themes can challenge students to see how the roles of director, actor, and stage designer can be tremendously innovative while understanding that Shakespeare's language gives clues to multiple interpretive possibilities.

3. Lessons for this act focus heavily on dramatic performance for three reasons: (a) students have gained greater confidence with Shakespeare's text by this point, allowing them to take performance risks; (b) authentic learning opportunities allow students to take on the roles and rituals of theater arts professionals, roles crucial to appreciating Shakespeare's text; and (c) Shakespeare's text is meant to be performed.

Handout 3.a.1: Mercurial Mercutio

A Workshop Presentation

Act 3, Scene 1

Actions	Text
Benvolio and Mercutio are at one side of the stage, talking. Benvolio turns and points at Tybalt as he says his line. Mercutio turns, too. Tybalt enters with a friend, stopping on the opposite side of the stage.	BENVOLIO: By my head, here comes the Capulets.
Mercutio turns his back to Tybalt and sticks his nose in the air.	MERCUTIO: By my heel, I care not.
Tybalt drops his hand on his friend's shoulder; they both cross the stage. Tybalt steps close to Benvolio and Mercutio. Mercutio pushes past Tybalt, knocking him back with his shoulder.	TYBALT: Follow me close, for I will speak to them. Gentlemen, good e'en. A word with one of you.
	MERCUTIO: And but one word with one of us? Couple it with something; make it a word and a blow.
Speaking to Mercutio's back.	TYBALT: You shall find me apt enough to that, sir, and you will give me occasion.
Looking at the audience, but smiling.	MERCUTIO: Could you not take some occasion without giving?
Trying to contain himself, trembling.	TYBALT: Mercutio, though consort'st with Romeo—
Turning to interrupt Tybalt. Pulls out sword. Benvolio steps forward and grabs Mercutio's sword arm. Tybalt takes a step	MERCUTIO: Consort! What, does thou make us minstrels? And thou makest minstrels of us, look to hear nothing but

back, but he also pulls out his sword.	discords. Here's my fiddle-stick; here's that shall make you dance. 'Zounds, consort!
Benvolio holds up both his hands, separating Mercutio and Tybalt.	BENVOLIO: We talk here in the public haunt of men: Either withdraw unto some private place, Or reason coldly of your grievances, Or else depart. Here all eyes gaze on us.
Mercutio pushes Benvolio's hands aside and points his sword at Tybalt.	MERCUTIO: Men's eyes were made to look, and let them gaze; I will not budge for no man's pleasure, I.

Teaching Romeo and Juliet: *A Differentiated Approach* by Delia DeCourcy, Lyn Fairchild, and Robin Follet © 2007 NCTE.

Lesson 3.b: Student Scenelets

Student Content and Skill Understandings

- Prepare to read and engage with a Shakespeare text. (AS)
- Summarize plot. (AS)
- Identify and explicate a character's traits using the character's actions, movements, speech, appearance, and reactions from other characters. (AS)
- Identify and explicate relationships between characters using the preceding elements. (OT/ADV)

Materials and Handouts

- 3.b.1: Suggested Scenelet Guide
- 3.b.2: Scenelet Templates A, B, and C
- 3.b.3: Presentation Rubric

Activities

STEP 1. TR Groups: Everyone's an Actor (10 minutes)

1. Ask students to discuss all the elements involved in blocking a scene when considering the placement of actors and their movement across a stage.

   a. NOV: How do the emotional motivations of characters determine character choices? How is balance of movement created on a stage? How are pace and momentum created? How can actors fully use the space? How, as with the use of camera angles, can levels and different heights be created to show superiority or inferiority, power or powerlessness?

   b. OT/ADV: How can balance, pace, and space emphasize certain themes? How does the evolution of emotions affect blocking? How can themes be represented by character choices?

2. Review the 3.b.3 Presentation Rubric and ask if students have any questions.

3. Break the class into small groups (see Notes on Differentiation about whether to assign groups or allow

student choice). Assign TR scenelets to groups based on the 3.b.1 Suggested Scenelet Guide. Use all or some of the suggested scenes. However, we advise that you cover the first series of suggested scenes: they address the sections of immediate importance.

STEP 2. TR Groups: Scenelet Preparations (40 minutes)

Ask all students to read through their assigned scenelets aloud, and then assign students to roles.

1. In the right-hand column of the template, have students write their lines. In the left-hand column, NOV students decide character actions; OT students decide character actions and blocking; and ADV students decide character actions, blocking, and the thematic texture that these create. **CHALLENGE:** incorporate at least one symbolic object within the scene that has not been mentioned in Shakespeare's text but that represents a motif.

2. After students complete their templates, ask them to practice the scene completely at least twice. Note: Students are not required to memorize their lines.

STEP 3. WCA: Review (5 minutes)

Review acting advice from the previous day's class. Students should be prepared to act their scenes in class the following day.

Epilogue: Suggested Homework

1. Encourage students to practice their lines and review decisions the group made in class.

2. Ask students to read selected scenes in act 3 and take notes as directed by you (key words and symbols) and/ or to make director's notes.

Notes on Differentiation

1. NOV students focus on comprehending lines and deciding on character emotions that lead to specific expressions, gestures, and movements, while OT students build on that foundation to analyze relationships between characters in this scene as shown by the blocking. ADV stu-

dents synthesize the acting and blocking to articulate a thematic argument for the "big ideas" happening on stage. Scenelets for NOV students contain high, more imaginable action, whereas OT/ADV scenes require greater reading comprehension, synthesis of disparate elements to create blocking, and understanding of character evolution within a scene.

2. Consider redefining what you mean by ADV if you have many strong actors in your class. Consult the Bardometer to recall students' interests in dramatic arts and then consider who has also impressed you or surprised you during class performances. For the purposes of this lesson, for example, ADV might mean a relatively strong reader with acting experience and stage presence. If you design MR groups, place ADV actors who are less skilled readers with one or more ADV readers who can explain the action and review word definitions with other group members. Then those ADV students in acting and blocking can take the scene and run with it. A group of ADV readers with little stage presence and acting confidence will not be able to make an ADV scenelet sophisticated.

3. If you prefer to allow student-selected groups, carefully explain all the challenges for levels A, B, and C. Let the students choose the level they find themselves ready for and encourage them not to choose groups based on friendships. The willingness to choose rigor based on their own readiness levels instead of choosing to be with peers is a habit that must be cultivated throughout the year.

3.b.1: Suggested Scenelet Guide

Act, Scene, and Line	Number of Students	Readiness Level
3.1.55–94 "Well, peace be with you . . . Courage, man . . ."	Four to eight students for Romeo, Benvolio, Mercutio, Tybalt, and assorted followers	NOV or OT
3.1.90–136 "A plague . . . O, I am Fortune's fool."	Five to eight students for Romeo, Benvolio, Mercutio, Tybalt, and Page	NOV or OT
3.5.68–104 "Madam, I am not well . . . But now I'll teach thee joyful tidings, girl."	Two students for Juliet and Lady Capulet	ADV
3.5.112–159 "Marry, my child . . . Hear me with patience but to speak a word."	Four students for Juliet, Lady Capulet, Lord Capulet, and the Nurse	OT
3.5.205–241 "O God . . . myself have the power to die."	Two students for Juliet and the Nurse	OT

Suggested Alternate Scenelets		
3.1.141–175 "Where are the vile . . . or let Benvolio die."	Six to eight students for the Prince, Montague, Lord Capulet, Lady Montague, Lady Capulet, Benvolio, and others	ADV: Although a number of characters are present in this scenelet, Benvolio has the most lines. The other characters must react to him appropriately.
3.1.176–198 "He is a kinsman . . . pardoning those that kill"	Three to eight students for the Prince, Lord Montague, Lord , Lady Montague, Lady Capulet, Benvolio, and others	OT: Again, the characters on stage must plan their reactions, even when they are not speaking.
3.2.61–95 "O Tybalt, Tybalt . . . to chide at him."	Two students for Juliet and the Nurse	NOV or OT
3.3.140–176 "A pack of blessings . . . Farewell."	Three students for the Nurse, Friar Laurence, and Romeo	NOV or OT
3.4.1–36 "Things have fall'n out . . . Good-night."	Three students for Lord Capulet, Lady Capulet, and Paris	OT
3.5.36–65 "More light and light . . . It is my lady Mother!"	Four students for Romeo, Juliet, the Nurse, and Lady Capulet	NOV

Handout 3.b.2: Scenelet Template A

Act 3, Scene _____, Lines _____ to _____.

Instructions:
1. Write the lines for your character in the Text area.
2. In the Acting area, write the actions that your character will perform when speaking or when others are speaking.

Acting (emotional motivation, gestures, movements, facial expressions, volume, pacing of speech)	**Text**

Teaching Romeo and Juliet: *A Differentiated Approach* by Delia DeCourcy, Lyn Fairchild, and Robin Follet © 2007 NCTE.

Handout 3.b.2: Scenelet Template B

Act 3, Scene _____ , **Lines** _____ **to** _____.

Instructions:

1. Write the lines for your character in the Text area.
2. In the Acting area, write the actions that your character will perform when speaking or when others are speaking.
3. In the Blocking area, make notes about where your character will move on stage in relation to other actors and props.

Acting (emotional motivation, gestures, movements, facial expressions, volume, pacing of speech)	**Blocking** (balance of actors on stage, movement across stage, pace of movement, use of full space)	**Text**

Teaching Romeo and Juliet: *A Differentiated Approach* by Delia DeCourcy, Lyn Fairchild, and Robin Follet © 2007 NCTE.

Handout 3.b.2: Scenelet Template C

Act 3, Scene _____, Lines _____ to _____.

Instructions:

1. Write the lines for your character in the Text area.
2. In the Acting area, write the actions that your character will perform when speaking or when others are speaking.
3. In the Blocking area, make notes about where your character will move on stage in relation to other actors and props.
4. In the Theme area, indicate the one or two themes that the choices in Acting and Blocking illustrate. Be prepared to justify to the class how your acting and blocking illustrate theme.

Theme (mood, tone, feeling, message)	Acting (emotional motivation, gestures, movements, facial expressions, volume, pacing of speech)	Blocking (balance of actors on stage, movement across stage, pace of movement, use of full space)	Text

Teaching Romeo and Juliet: *A Differentiated Approach* by Delia DeCourcy, Lyn Fairchild, and Robin Follet © 2007 NCTE.

Handout 3.b.3: Presentation Rubric

Names of group members:

1. **Acting:** Effort at and quality of acting when not speaking

   INCOMPLETE   COMPETENT   SOPHISTICATED

2. **Acting:** Creativity in two or more of the following: emotional motivation, gestures, movements, facial expressions, volume, and/or pacing of speech

   INCOMPLETE   COMPETENT   SOPHISTICATED

3. **Blocking:** Balance of actors on stage, movement across stage, pace of movement; use of full space (if assigned)

   INCOMPLETE   COMPETENT   SOPHISTICATED

4. **Themes:** Use of acting and blocking to represent a theme (if assigned)

   INCOMPLETE   COMPETENT   SOPHISTICATED

5. **Flow, Unity, and Preparedness:** Evidence that the group has practiced several times

   INCOMPLETE   COMPETENT   SOPHISTICATED

Lesson 3.c: Scenelet Presentations

Student Content and Skill Understandings

- Prepare to read and engage with a Shakespeare text. (AS)
- Summarize plot. (AS)
- Identify and explicate a character's traits using the character's actions, movements, speech, appearance, and reactions from other characters. (AS)
- Identify and explicate relationships between characters using the preceding elements. (OT/ADV)

Materials and Handouts

- 3.b.3: Presentation Rubric handout (see page 216)
- 3.c.1: Journals A, B, and C handout

Activities

STEP 1. WCA: Scenelets (50 minutes)

1. Ask students to present their partial scenes sequentially. ADV presenters can provide a one-minute explanation of how acting and blocking illustrated themes in action.
2. Applaud all the actors after their efforts. Ask students to comment on the best aspects of each performance, with specific references to acting, blocking, and theme.
3. For each scenelet, use the handout 3.b.3: Presentation Rubric to assess the performance.

Epilogue: Suggested Homework

Assign TR journals, asking students to respond to one of the questions, based on their understanding of act 3 and the student scenelets. In addition, students can use the skill strand activities to explore their areas of interest within *Romeo and Juliet* (see page 221).

Notes on Differentiation

1. As with scenelets, consider letting students choose which journal level they would like to attempt.

2. If you would like to develop close readers for this act, consider using Juliet's soliloquy from scene 2 or the entire scene; an excerpt of Friar Laurence's counseling of Romeo and his dialogue with him before the Nurse enters in scene 3, or just Friar Laurence's upbraiding of Romeo ("Hold thy desperate hand!"); scene 5 between Romeo and Juliet before the Nurse enters; and/or Capulet's rant against Juliet ("God's bread, it makes me mad") to the end of the scene.

3. ADV students can develop CRs for other students as part of a compacting project, and all students can be encouraged to select among the scenes listed above to complete one close reading during the study of act 3. Emphasize once again the use of the Tips for Tackling the Language handout, the creation of symbolic illustrations or written summaries, and the highlighting of key words (abstract nouns, adjectives, and verbs) that represent any of the themes studied thus far.

4. Use creative writing, cinematic, dramatic, or Socratic discussion skill strand activities to plan remaining lessons for act 3, as well as assigning end-of-unit or ongoing projects. By the end of act 3, you may want to break up the weekly rhythm by allowing half a class period once a week or one day a week for project time, especially if students will be working in groups and performing.

Handout 3.c.1: Journals A, B, and C

Act 3 Journals A

1. Why would Romeo not want to fight Tybalt? Do you agree or disagree with his choice?

2. Why does Mercutio get angry? Do you support Mercutio's reasons for listening to his own anger? What do you think of his choices?

3. How has Romeo's love for Juliet affected his behavior in this scene?

4. Do you sympathize with Romeo in his position of being banished? Why or why not?

5. Why are Juliet's parents angry with her? Do you sympathize with their feelings toward her? Why or why not?

6. Should Juliet listen to the Nurse's advice and forget Romeo? Why or why not? What would you do in her position?

Act 3 Journals B

1. Who is responsible for the fight? Why?

2. Should Romeo be banished or killed for the murder of Tybalt, or should another punishment be considered? What punishment would you propose? Why?

3. Why do Juliet's parents and the Nurse behave the way they do? Step into their shoes and justify their actions.

4. How has Western society changed since Juliet's day (we can assume the 1590s, when this play was written) when it comes to love and marriage? Compare her situation to a modern-day girl's.

5. What choices does Juliet have right now? List all of her options and then select the option you feel is best for her; justify your reasoning.

Act 3 Journals C

1. Who is responsible for the fight? Why? Who is responsible for the death of Mercutio? Why? If you believe

multiple characters are responsible for the fight and the death, explain who is the most and who is the least responsible and why, and define the criteria you are using for these judgments.

2. How has Juliet's or any other character's identity changed in this act? Give specifics. To what do you attribute this change in identity?

3. Where is the theme of dichotomy and paradox most evident in act 3? Why?

4. Could a modern-day Juliet be caught in the same difficult circumstances regarding marriage? Think of parallels to today's pressures and explain your comparison.

5. What choices does Juliet have right now? List all of her options and rank them on a scale of 1 to 5, 1 being the best and 5 being the worst. To consider: How much risk could she handle? Can a choice be wise and still be risky? Can a choice be good and still be immoral (such as lying to one's parents in order to marry the one she loves)?

Skill Strands

Creative Writing

The Argument Is in the Silence

The tension in an argument often grows from how people react combined with what they say. When Tybalt accosts Romeo in act 3, Juliet's new husband denies Tybalt's insult of "villain." He says, "Villain am I none." Then Romeo attempts to turn aside the argument with soft words and polite actions. His attempts fail.

Shakespeare understood how to create believable characters with specific motivations for fighting or not fighting. He also knew how to create tension in a scene: let people work their way toward the screaming match or the swordplay rather than begin with fists swinging. A writer should generally avoid having his characters yelling at the beginning of a conversation; they should also avoid pulling out swords when they first meet.

Here's your mission: create a dialogue that builds slowly toward a screaming match, a physical fight, or some other dramatic conflict.

Brainstorming

1. First, brainstorm situations in which one person is angry with another. Create interesting motivations for one of these characters to be angry with the other. Who are these people? What occurred before this scene between the two?

2. Second, in list form, write some of the details about these characters. Are they natural fighters or peacemakers? Are they skilled at arguing? At physical combat?

3. Third, decide the climax: what will one character say or do to another? Remember, the climax does not necessarily have to be an act of violence. The character decisions should be determined by their personalities, motivations, history together, and also by their response to the other character's decisions in the scene.

Writing

Write the first paragraph. Introduce the characters, the setting, and the situation. Then:

1. In the second paragraph, the two characters briefly talk with each other. Remember: they should not be yelling at this point.

2. In the third paragraph, have a **denial** occur. Then have a character's action demonstrate his or her anger. It shouldn't be obvious: George shouldn't smack Ralph in the face. Make it **subtle**.

3. In the next few paragraphs, mix actions with words. Actions should show the characters trying to avoid the confrontation, but then finally giving into the anger.

4. End the dialogue with an angry statement followed by a decisive action.

Glossary:
denial: a refusal to believe or accept
subtle: evident through small clues and hints

Cinema

Which Fight Do You Prefer?

The depiction of the fight scene in which Mercutio and Tybalt both die is quite different in the Luhrmann and Zeffirelli versions. Watch both versions of this important scene. Make a comparison chart that considers the following:

Element	Zeffirelli	Luhrmann
Location of fight		
Costumes		
Weapons used		
Role of Mercutio		
Location of Mercutio's death		
How does Romeo chase Tybalt?		
Nature of the fight between Romeo and Tybalt		

Role of the crowd in the scene		
What do you notice about the atmosphere—dust, sand, heat?		
Lines emphasized		
Lines cut		

Socratic Discussion

Love and Marriage: Play-Related Questions

- Consider Romeo's and Juliet's behaviors in this act. Do they indicate a strong commitment to marriage? Why or why not? Which of the lovers seems more committed to the impending marriage? Why?

Love and Marriage: Relevance Questions

- What responsibility do husbands and wives have to each other? What sacrifices are appropriate? What sacrifices are too extreme in a marriage?

Rebellion: Play-Related Questions

- In act 3, scene 5, Juliet rebels against her father's wishes by refusing to marry Paris. How is this refusal a rebellion not only against his power, but also against the structure and norms of Elizabethan society?
- Why would Juliet take such a risk?

Rebellion: Relevance Questions

- In what situations might children feel motivated to rebel against their parents? Are those rebellions effective? Why or why not?

Dichotomy and Paradox: **Play-Related Questions**

- How can Juliet both hate and love Romeo after he kills Tybalt?

Dichotomy and Paradox: **Relevance Questions**

- When might people find themselves feeling both love and hate for someone? What kinds of relationships tend to elicit such opposing feelings?

Identity: **Play-Related Questions**

- Why is death better than banishment, according to Romeo? What do you think of Romeo's attitude? What do we learn about his personality and identity in this scene?
- How does this newly formed bond change Romeo and Juliet? Does each of the young lovers think differently about their future now?

Identity: **Relevance Questions**

- How do people's sense of identity change when they get married? Should it change?

Motifs: **Play-Related Questions**

- *Interior and exterior*: Explore where each scene in act 3 occurs. What action takes place in the public square? In the privacy of the Friar's cell? Inside the Capulet household? How is the location of these actions and decisions significant?
- *Night and day, light and dark*: In act 3, scene 5, Romeo and Juliet argue over whether it is the nightingale or the lark singing outside the window. What do these two birds symbolize both in nature and in the larger picture of the play?
- *Looking and sight*: Romeo, Mercutio, Juliet, and Lord Capulet all have experiences in this act in which they realize that things or people are not as they appeared. Consider the moments in act 3 when these characters see a person or a situation in a different light. What brings about this altered vision?

- *Masks*: Juliet begins to transform in this act. What are the "masks" she wears in act 3 as she attempts to conceal her new role as Romeo's wife from her father and mother, as well as her desire to take charge of her future as she talks to the Nurse?

- *Time: haste v. slowness*: Where in this act are events decided more quickly than others? Why? What do you think of the characters' judgments in these scenes?

Motifs: Relevance Questions

- *Interior and exterior*: How does location affect how you behave? Are you a "different person" in public compared to the person you are in private?

- *Night and day, light and dark*: What connotations do words and images like *night* and *day*, *light* and *dark*, have?

- *Looking and sight*: Consider a time when you began to "see" a person close to you differently. What prompted that change in "vision"?

- *Masks*: Often people behave differently when they are with one group of people versus another group. Is this dishonest behavior—or merely a necessary habit for survival and therefore appropriate?

- *Time: haste v. slowness*: What happens to your sense of judgment when you make decisions hastily?

Name_____ Period_____

Act 3 Reading Quiz

1. How does Mercutio judge Benvolio's character?
   a. Benvolio is a calm man who never fights.
   b. Benvolio is a man who will fight for no good reason.
   c. Benvolio will fight only when he has a good reason.
   d. Benvolio will start a fight, but then he will run away.

2. Why does Mercutio fight with Tybalt?
   a. Tybalt hits Mercutio.
   b. Mercutio is standing up for Romeo's honor.
   c. Romeo tells Mercutio to fight.
   d. Benvolio starts the fight and Mercutio joins it.

3. Why does Romeo fight with Tybalt?
   a. Benvolio starts the fight and Romeo joins it.
   b. Romeo fights him to take revenge for Mercutio's death.
   c. Benvolio tells Romeo to fight.
   d. Tybalt hits Romeo.

4. Why does Juliet claim that the singing bird is a nightingale rather than a lark?
   a. The nightingale represents the evening, meaning that Romeo can stay.
   b. The nightingale represents the dawn, meaning that Romeo can stay.
   c. The lark is a traditional symbol of evil.
   d. The Nurse has a pet lark, who sings whenever she walks into Juliet's room.

5. How does Lady Capulet offer to have Romeo killed?
   a. Hire a man to slip him poison.
   b. Hire a man to stab him.
   c. Let Count Paris fight him.
   d. Have him hanged in the public square.

6. When Lord Capulet learns that Juliet refuses to marry Count Paris, how does he react?

   a. He embraces her because he agrees with her decision.

   b. He fires the Nurse because he feels it was her job to convince Juliet to marry the Count.

   c. He yells at his wife, calling her ugly names.

   d. He shouts at Juliet, calling her ugly names.

7. What advice does the Nurse offer Juliet?

   a. Forget Romeo and marry Count Paris.

   b. Run away from home to be with Romeo.

   c. Pretend to die, and then Romeo will rescue you from the grave.

   d. Ask Friar Laurence for guidance.

8. "A plague o' both your houses" means that

   a. Tybalt has brought diseases to both the Montague and Capulet households.

   b. Because of the black plague, the houses of Montague and Capulet will be closed.

   c. Romeo has brought diseases to both the Montague and Capulet households.

   d. The houses of Montague and Capulet are placed under a curse by Tybalt.

9. "Ask for me tomorrow, and you shall find me a grave man" is an example of

   a. Irony

   b. An oxymoron

   c. A pun

   d. A simile

10. When Romeo is discussing his punishment with Friar Laurence, Romeo states, "Calling death 'banished' / Thou cutt'st my head off with a golden axe, / And smil'st upon the stroke that murders me." What does Romeo mean?

a. Friar Laurence is threatening Romeo with a golden axe.

b. By treating Romeo's banishment as a positive situation, the Friar has the mistaken belief that life without Juliet will be bearable for Romeo.

c. Romeo prefers death to being with Juliet.

d. Because Juliet is making mean statements about Romeo, he feels as though he is being killed.

5 Act 4: Lessons, Activities, and Handouts

Act 4, Scene 1

Lesson 4.a: Do I Have To?

Student Content and Skill Understandings

- Prepare to read and engage with a Shakespeare text: summarize, define, predict, translate, highlight. (AS)
- Summarize plot, identify narrative structure, and explain cause-and-effect relationships orally and in writing; predict plot outcomes based on narrative structure. (AS)
- Know the definition of irony and apply it to plot events (AS)
- Know features of Shakespeare's language (blank verse, subtext, and iambic pentameter). (AS)
- Scan Shakespeare's lines. (OT/ADV)
- Analyze and evaluate in writing a character's motivations, choices, and consequences according to themes. (OT/ADV)

Themes

- Love and marriage
- Rebellion
- Time: haste v. slowness

Materials and Handouts

- 4.a.1: How Many Ways Can You Say Goodbye? handout

Activities

STEP 1. OPTIONAL. WCA: Journal Writing and Sharing (15 minutes)

1. Option 1: See the end of act 4 for journal prompts on themes listed above.

2. Option 2: Provide a definition of *irony* for students and ask them to write about a time when events in their lives turned out contrary to expectations: When in your life did the firehouse catch on fire? When did someone who was supposed to be your role model act hypocritically? When did you not fulfill the expectations of a role and ended up doing the opposite? When did you realize that you had the same behaviors as your enemy? You may also have to clarify the difference between irony and bad luck. See Notes on Differentiation for more tips on teaching irony.

STEP 2. WCA and MR Groups: Script Improvisations and "Stressing Out": How Many Ways Can You Say Goodbye? (30 minutes)

1. OPTIONAL: Tell students that the scene they will study today is the one in which Juliet and Paris meet for the first time with Friar Laurence. If you chose to have students write about irony, ask them to talk about all the ways in which the first meeting between two engaged people and the person who is supposed to marry them could be ironic. How do we expect the two engaged people to behave? How do we expect the person who will marry them to behave? Then, how might they behave in ways that are contrary to expectations?

2. Explain to students that they are at the point of being able to not only translate character dialogue but also understand the hidden messages that are sent when a character speaks. Explain that scene 1 of act 4 is powerful because of the subtext of Juliet and the Friar's conversation. The readers and spectators know of Juliet's secret love, while Paris does not. Define *subtext* as the words beneath a character's dialogue that represent any feelings not being shared, otherwise known as the interior monologue inside that character's head. Subtext (internal emotional state) hides behind the text (external emotional state) or the "face" a character puts on. You can discuss the prefix *sub* as well as synonyms such as implicit versus explicit and hidden versus revealed.

3. Ask students to brainstorm situations or relationships in which people tend not to say what they feel and to instead

hide their emotions. When are people afraid, reluctant, or unable to speak their minds? (Suggestions: during a job interview; during a first date; during a traffic stop by a police officer; during a conversation with one's parents when you've done something wrong; during a class when all your peers are listening to what you're saying.)

4. Ask students to identify five different potential subtextual meanings behind the ordinary greeting "Hello." Draw (or have a student draw) five stick figures on a board or overhead with a cartoon bubble of "Hello" coming from their mouths. Then draw five thought bubbles and brainstorm a different emotion for each stick figure. Ask students to imagine situations between two or more people in which these emotions might appear in an opening line of "Hello." When would someone be angry at hello? Nervous? Suggestions: a parent and child meeting after a long absence; a romantic partner attracted to the other, indicating that she or he is pleased with how the other person looks; a romantic partner angry with the other, who is late—again; two enemies passing and mocking each other; a job candidate trying to impress the potential boss during an interview. Ask students to say the word *hello* in these situations and then listen to where the stress falls—on "hel" or "lo" (emphasis and inflection)? How quickly is each syllable said (speed)? How loudly or softly (volume)?

5. MR Pairs, Triads, or Quads: Distribute the 4.a.1: How Many Ways Can You Say Goodbye? handout and review the directions.

6. Have students perform different scenarios without announcing the characters' jobs, conflicts, or settings. Have the students in the audience guess what these are.

7. Encourage students to compliment other groups' creative choices and discuss how the performers used the performance skills of emphasis, inflection, speed, and volume to indicate subtext.

STEP 3. WCA: Reading Comprehension and Rehearsal with TR Questions (20 minutes)

1. Explain to students that they will be reading and analyzing the opening of act 4, scene 1, applying the lessons from How Many Ways Can You Say Goodbye?

2. Define any necessary terms such as *confession* and *slander* and establish context for the scene.

3. Find three actors from the class who are willing to read and perform the scene from the Friar's opening line through Juliet's line "It may be so . . ." Ask Tips for Tackling the Language questions while the students read these lines through at least twice.

4. Allow the students to perform the scene a third time.

5. After the performance, ask TR questions about the lines that begin with Paris ("Happily met . . .") through Juliet's line "It may be so . . ."

    a. NOV: What words indicate emotions or feelings that characters are freely expressing? Who speaks most of them? How are Paris's emotions different from Juliet's?

    b. NOV/OT: What adjectives could describe each character's—Paris and Juliet—external or revealed emotional state and attitude here? How do you know? What about each character's internal or hidden emotional state—the subtext? Where in her dialogue does Juliet hint at her true meaning?

    c. OT/ADV: If you were directing the actors for Juliet and Paris, what words would you emphasize to let the subtext emerge? Why? What other techniques that you used in your improvisational skits would apply here? What emotions might Friar Laurence be feeling? How do you know? How should he speak?

Notes on Differentiation

1. When teaching the concept of irony, you might want to use lyrics from the much-discussed song by Alanis Morissette, "Isn't It Ironic," a song that contains some examples of irony but more of bad luck or coincidental situations. "Rain on your wedding day" is not ironic since many weddings occur on rainy days, much to the bride's chagrin, and it's not a surprise with a bitter twist. How-

ever, a person waiting his whole life to fly on a plane due to a phobia and then that one plane trip ending in a crash *is* irony. Students can then pinpoint which situations in *Romeo and Juliet* are fateful versus ironic and which are both.

2. Giving students time to slowly read the text and play with improvisation not only allows them to review core skills for close reading but also helps students see the complexity of emotions in Shakespeare's scenes using a concept from their own experience—subtext.

3. You can change the MR activity How Many Ways Can You Say Goodbye? to TR groups if you prefer, and limit NOV students to a certain number of subtext skills (emphasis and speed, for example). Note that your groupings for this activity should not be based on reading level but on acting ability, so NOV students are those "least likely to be found on a stage," while your ADV students are "total hams." This activity also has the potential to take an entire period if you wish to further emphasize the concept of subtext.

4. For another take on how to teach subtext in *Romeo and Juliet*, see lessons in the Folger Library's *Shakespeare Set Free*. This lesson guide provides several good dramatic skill strand activities.

Epilogue: Suggested Homework

If students show a readiness to handle scanning on their own, assign the handouts from the following lesson for homework: 4.b.1: Five Stresses Are All You've Got and 4.b.2: Shakescholar Close Readers A, B, and C (pages 244–57).

Handout 4.a.1: How Many Ways Can You Say Goodbye?

Directions

Your goal is to create two or three different scenes that have the same text (see the separate script handout) but two or three different subtexts. You will choose between two possible scripts or create your own.

1. Form groups of two or more students (no more than four).

2. Read the script aloud as a group three different times. Each time you read, emphasize a different word or syllable for each character's line so you can hear different possibilities.

3. Brainstorm two or three different scenarios in which this same script could be used. What double meanings could these sentences have? Vary the characters, the plot, the setting, and, most important, the way you say the words. You must choose the characters, the setting, and the conflict.

4. Every group member must be used in the scene. If a person isn't speaking, he or she should play a secondary, silent character to set the scene, such as pantomiming that he or she is a patron in a coffee shop.

5. Note that there is no end punctuation in the script. Add your own for each new scene.

6. Tools to help you deliver these lines include the following:

   - Emphasis: saying a word or a syllable of a word more loudly and strongly. Think about the sentence "I love you." What is the difference between saying, "I love you" versus "I *love* you" versus "I love *you*"? Or how about the word *impossible*: does a character say, "Im-possible!" or "Imp*ossi*ble!"?

   - Inflection: bringing the pitch of your voice up or down for effect. How high or low should your voice be on a certain word or syllable?

   - Rest: waiting before or after a word for effect, as in music when there are "rests" in between notes.

   - Speed: hastening or slowing phrases or words for effect.

- Volume: loudness or softness of the voice (do remember that actors must be loud enough to be heard). How loudly or softly should certain sentences, phrases, words, or syllables be spoken?
- Articulation: emphasizing multiple syllables as clearly as possible for effect.
- Body language: using nonverbal communication—gestures, posture, eye contact.
- Space: the set, the props, and any other physical items you can use.

A few thoughts on character, setting, and conflict:

Character: Give each character a name, an age, and a job.

Setting: Give the location a specific description (e.g., physical space, region/state, time of day). Setting includes geography and time. We will assume that you are setting the scene in the current year.

Conflict: Give each character a different desire (want) in this scene that would cause a conflict. If possible, you might also want to imagine a history between the two people of repeatedly conflicting wants.

A few thoughts on punctuation:

Question mark: indicates doubt, curiosity, and/or wonder

Exclamation point: indicates a strong emotion and often a loud voice

Period: indicates the end of a thought, when a person takes a breath

Ellipsis: indicates a person's voice trailing off because the person is unable, for whatever reason, to finish his or her thought

Dash: indicates a person is still talking and will be interrupted by the following speaker

Teaching Romeo and Juliet: *A Differentiated Approach* by Delia DeCourcy, Lyn Fairchild, and Robin Follet © 2007 NCTE.

How Many Ways Can You Say Goodbye? The Script

Script 1

Person 1: That is it

Person 2: Is that all the boxes

Person 1: I think so

Person 2: Goodbye

Person 1: Bye

Person 2: Wait, you forgot this

Person 1: I did

Script 2

Person 1: Are those the boxes

Person 2: What do you mean

Person 1: The boxes

Person 2: Oh those

Person 1: Those

Person 2: Well, that's it

Person 1: You don't say

CHALLENGE: Create your own script and use it instead of the ones above.

Brainstorm situations that would fit these lines and practice each scene you create.

Scene 1: Character names, ages, and jobs: _____

_____

Setting: _____

._____

Conflict: _____

_____

Scene 2: Character names, ages, and jobs: _____

_____

Setting: _____

_____

Conflict: _____

_____

Scene 3: Character names, ages, and jobs: _____

_____

Setting: _____

_____

Conflict: _____

_____

Teaching Romeo and Juliet: *A Differentiated Approach* by Delia DeCourcy, Lyn Fairchild, and Robin Follet © 2007 NCTE.

Lesson 4.b: Do I Have To?

Student Content and Skill Understandings

- Prepare to read and engage with a Shakespeare text: summarize, define, predict, translate, highlight. (AS)
- Summarize plot, identify narrative structure, and explain cause-and-effect relationships orally and in writing; predict plot outcomes based on narrative structure. (AS)
- Know features of Shakespeare's language (blank verse and iambic pentameter). (AS)
- Scan Shakespeare's lines. (OT/ADV)
- Analyze and evaluate in writing a character's motivations, choices, and consequences according to themes. (OT/ADV)

Themes

- Love and marriage
- Rebellion
- Time: haste v. slowness

Materials and Handouts

- 4.b.1: Five Stresses Are All You've Got handout
- 4.b.2: Shakescholar Close Readers A, B, and C
- Props
- Film versions of the play directed by Franco Zeffirelli and Baz Luhrmann

Activities

STEP 1. OPTIONAL. WCA: Mini-Lesson: Five Stresses Are All You've Got (15 minutes)

See the 4.b.1: Five Stresses Are All You've Got handout.

STEP 2. MR Pairs: Scanning and Rehearsing (15 minutes)

1. Ask students to form MR pairs and take the role of directors reviewing a script in order to prepare how they will direct this scene between Paris and Juliet. To

show the strength of both Paris's and Juliet's emotions, they will use the strategy of emphasis. They will mark words or syllables in the play text with a slash mark where they want Paris or Juliet to stress their words with emotion. They may use no more than five or six slash marks, or stresses, per line. As they work, they should check the emphasis by reading it aloud, asking themselves: *Are the emotions authentically represented by the emphasis? Is the emphasis realistic to human speech?*

2. Ask some pairs to demonstrate how they would read the scene with these new emphases.

3. Ask the class to discuss why these student directors might have placed the stresses where they did. How do the stresses reflect the emotions the characters are feeling?

4. OPTIONAL. Ask students to report on their findings about ironic actions and behaviors in the scene. Did Juliet and Paris act like typical young people who are engaged to be married—in an arranged situation? Did Friar Laurence act like a typical religious role model? What might be Shakespeare's point in showing some of these ironies?

STEP 3. TR Groups: Scanning and Rehearsing (30 minutes)

Have students complete 4.b.2: Shakescholar Close Readers A, B, and C for act 4, scene 1, from the opening line until Juliet's line, "To live an unstain'd wife . . ."

Epilogue: Suggested Homework

Read Juliet's soliloquy in scene 3, lines 20–58, in which she contemplates the vial of potion she must take to feign her death. Options to assign for analysis, based on your perception of student readiness, include completing a scene summary of every 5–10 lines; scanning the lines, circling key words that are emphasized for thematic emphasis, and listing those themes; or writing a few paragraphs about how the motifs of nature and night emphasize larger themes in the play.

Students can also follow their interests in using the skill strand assignments on pages 258–60.

Notes on Differentiation

1. Five Stresses Are All You've Got can also be taught as a mini-lesson to OT and ADV groups during the TR groups for CRs, as NOV students will not focus on scanning skills.

2. If as a group your students show readiness to implement subtext skills beyond emphasis, encourage them to further mark up the Shakespeare texts with indications of rest, speed, body language, and so forth. They can also develop "director's marks," a code to indicate what they visualize and hear for each line of dialogue. Students should be familiar with electronic emoticons in the online world that can be used to express emotions; they can create symbols for emphasis, volume, speed, and so forth.

3. CRs differ in this way: NOV students answer questions about thematic references to time and directorial emphasis for some lines while reading more text than OT students; OT students search for subtext, complete the Five Stresses Are All You've Got handout, scan the text to decide how it can emphasize Juliet's subtext, and then answer questions about thematic references; ADV students scan, analyze a selection of text, complete the handout, analyze the implications of broken scansion and split-level lines, compare this scene to act 1, scene 5 where Romeo and Juliet first meet, and have the option to trace Juliet's character evolution since act 1. Note that CR C (ADV) may be too complex if your ADV students don't understand subtext after the WCA, so assign this one only if they have mastered the concept of subtext; otherwise, just use CRs A and B. You will note that OT students are doing line-by-line analysis at this stage because, at this point in the reading of the play, they should be reading not just lines but "between them" in preparation for commentary on evidence when they are essay writing. The hope is that ADV students are naturally close readers and do not need as much scaffolding for the commentary on evidence. NOV students are not given this preparation, as their reading skills are still being developed for basic plot and characterization.

4. If you have emphasized iambic pentameter previous to act 4, you can use the term more freely in this lesson.

5. Other scenes from act 4 that you can develop CRs for or take time in class to discuss: Juliet's soliloquy in the scene that begins with "Farewell! God knows . . ." and an excerpt of scene 5 when Juliet is discovered "dead," beginning with the Nurse's "O woe!" until the end of the Friar's speech.

6. Skill strand assignments are options for long-term projects (refer to act 3's skill strand assignments to see project ideas).

Chapter 5

Handout 4.b.1: Five Stresses Are All You've Got

Fact: Shakespeare's lines have about ten beats, or syllables, per line.
Try It: Find a passage in act 4, scene 1 of four lines; count the number of syllables per line.

Fact: Sometimes Shakespeare goes over or under ten beats, but never by many.
Try It: When film director Baz Luhrmann turned *Romeo and Juliet* into a film, he had the lines of the Prologue read by a modern newscaster. Why? Because if you listen to the number of words the human breath can handle in an average one- to two-sentence delivery, you will hear iambic pentameter. Therefore, the opening lines of a TV news report can often be quite rhythmic. Take the role of newscaster for a minute and write the copy you will read for the news. Write a two- to three-sentence introduction on the following topics with ten syllables per line:

- The opening lines to an evening news report on any current events topic; example 1:

   "Today in the suburbs of Westin Town /
   police pulled up to Brenda Smith's garage /
   and sadly witnessed a heartbreaking scene."

   or example 2 (a news report on a modern-day version of a *Romeo and Juliet* news event):

   Police arrived in York's town square tonight, /
   too late to stop the violence between youths /
   of brutal gun-slinging gangs known for feuds.

- The opening line of your speech accepting an award you hope to win someday

- The lines of sports commentary during a high-stakes athletic contest

Discuss: Was it easy or hard to limit yourself to ten beats per line? Why or why not?

Fact: Shakespeare used this rhythm structure, called unrhymed *iambic pentameter*, or *blank verse*, in most scenes of most of his plays. Let's break down these words:

   iamb: An iamb is a two-beat, or two-syllable, section of a line. In an iamb, the first beat is unstressed and the second beat is stressed. An iamb is like the human heartbeat: Thud-THUD.

Try It: Read the sentences you created above, using your pencil, hands, or feet to tap, clap, or stomp out the rhythm. If the words or syllables that are stressed aren't that important, what words or phrases do you need to change? Note that in example 2, stresses fall on key words such as *youths*, *gun*, and *known*.

> *Pentameter*: *Penta* means "five" (think pentagon, five sides), and *meter* means "rhythm," or the number of beats per line. Poets also call the iamb a metric foot, because back in the days of the ancient Greek choruses, the actors in the chorus would walk one step for each syllable until they came to the end of a line. Then they turned to walk back across the stage.

Fact: When you scan a line, you mark the iambic pentameter like this (here, during Romeo and Juliet's balcony scene, Romeo first sees Juliet):

But sóft/ what líght/ through yón/ der wín/ dow bréaks?

Note how key words like *soft*, *light*, and *breaks* receive the emphasis. Romeo's emotions emerge on those words, and those words represent thematic concepts. *Soft* means "wait," and these lovers have trouble waiting. *Light* is a common motif that Romeo uses to compare to Juliet, and *breaks* has the connotation of fighting and dueling, which is the backdrop against which this romance is set.

Try It: Note how we have scanned Friar Laurence's first line in act 4, scene 1, the same way we scanned Romeo's line. Circle the syllables where the stresses fall in each iamb.

On Thúrs/ day, sír?/ the tíme/ is vé/ ry shórt.

Discuss: What words or syllables are stressed? Discuss with your peers how the syllable stresses and play themes relate.

Try It: Now rewrite the news report lines you wrote earlier. Search for synonyms and rearrange words to express the same thoughts in iambic pentameter so that there are not only ten syllables but also stresses on as many second syllables or words that matter.

Teaching Romeo and Juliet: *A Differentiated Approach* by Delia DeCourcy, Lyn Fairchild, and Robin Follet © 2007 NCTE.

Handout 4.b.2: Shakescholar Close Reader A

Act 4, Scene 1, Lines _____ – _____

From the Friar's line "On Thursday, sir?" to the Friar's line "On Thursday next . . ."

> *Facilitator*: Reads directions and keeps the group on task. Leads the discussion about what symbol should be used (see Symbolist role).
>
> *Reader*: Reads the text aloud, stopping when the Explicator asks.
>
> *Explicator*: Leads group in translating the lines, stopping the Reader every few lines. Everyone should assist the Explicator, using the Tips for Tackling the Language handout.
>
> *Researcher*: Uses the book references, a dictionary, or a glossary to define words that the whole group does not know. Everyone should assist the Researcher.
>
> *Symbolist*: Designs an easy-to-draw symbol that will help everyone remember the events of the plot up to a certain line.

You will need your Tips for Tackling the Language handout.

To Read:

1. Choose group roles.
2. Open your books to act 4, scene 1, line 1. You will need the references in the text.
3. Listen to the Reader read the first five lines of text on this handout.
4. Help the Explicator translate and help the Researcher provide references using your handout and book.
5. Have the Facilitator lead a discussion to propose a symbol for the first five lines.
6. Have the Symbolist draw it and everyone copy it on their close readers.
7. Proceed through the rest of the text in this manner, explicating and drawing after every sixth line. When you have finished, complete the next steps: To Read Closely.

Plot Summary:

In the opening lines, Paris shares with Friar Laurence that he and Juliet will wed in two days and that Juliet can't stop crying because of Tybalt's death. Paris reports that Lord Capulet thinks Juliet will do better having company (by being married) than crying and being alone, consumed by her thoughts. Friar Laurence says things are moving too fast. Juliet enters and Paris tells her he is happy to see her and ready to be married. Juliet replies as though she agrees with him but does not express any love. She speaks in double meanings. She asks the Friar if he has time for confession, and the Friar asks Paris to leave. Once Paris is gone, Juliet cries that she is desperate, past help, and the Friar sympathizes with her.

To Read Closely: (Use a pencil for this part)

1. Underline or write all the words in the opening lines between the Friar and Paris that deal with the theme of time: haste versus slowness. Put a slash mark above those words. Remember that you don't have to mark a whole word but can mark a syllable.

2. Read aloud those lines so that the time words are given special emphasis.

3. Read from Juliet's entrance to her line "It may be so . . ." and put slash marks over words or syllables. You will do this three different times. Then:

   a. Pretend that the actress who plays Juliet has a cue from her director to play the role as very NERVOUS or ANXIOUS. Put slash marks over the words or syllables that will help the actress do so.

   b. Pretend that the actress has been asked by her director to play the role as IRATE, or ANGRY. Add new slash marks where necessary.

   c. Now discuss which slash marks to keep by considering these questions:

      - Can Juliet be both anxious and angry at the same time? Would she be more anxious than angry, or vice versa? Would her emotions change between her entrance and her final words to Paris?

      - You can have only five stresses, or beats, per line. Erase those that are not as effective and keep

   those that emphasize the emotion(s) you think
   Juliet is feeling most strongly.

4. Read Juliet's words to the Friar beginning with "O shut
   the door . . ." What is Juliet feeling? Place five stresses or
   beats per line to emphasize emotions.

5. Discuss as a group what you think Juliet's options are
   right now.

   a. Suggest at least four options for Juliet.

   b. Whatever option Juliet chooses, it will be rushed be-
      cause otherwise she will be married to a man she
      doesn't love in two days. How might the rush affect
      her final choice? What choice do you think Juliet will
      make? Why?

   c. Choose the option you think is the best for her, what
      Juliet *should* do (rather than what she might actually
      do).

6. Show the teacher what you have accomplished. If your
   group is enjoying the scene and has good ideas for blocking and directing it, ask the teacher if you can practice
   and perform it later for the class.

7. Predict three possible outcomes from the choices Juliet
   might make:

Prediction 1	Prediction 2	Prediction 3

Handout 4.b.2: Shakescholar Close Reader B

Act 4, Scene 1, Lines _____ – _____

From the Friar's line "On Thursday, sir?" to Juliet's line "It may be so . . ."

Facilitator: Reads directions and keeps the group on task.

Reader: Reads the text aloud, stopping when the Explicator asks.

Explicator: Leads group in translating the lines, stopping the Reader every few lines. Everyone should assist the Explicator, using the Tips for Tackling the Language handout.

Researcher: Uses the book references, a dictionary, or a glossary to define words that the whole group does not know. Everyone should assist the Researcher.

Summarizer: Leads the discussion about what summary should represent the plot up until the last line discussed; creates a list of words, a brief phrase, or even a topic sentence to summarize the group's agreement.

You will need your Tips for Tackling the Language handout.

To Read Closely:

1. Choose group roles and open your books to act 4, scene 1, line 1.

2. Have the Reader read the first 6–8 lines of text in the scene.

3. Have the Explicator translate and the Researcher provide references.

4. Have the Summarizer lead a discussion on an appropriate set of words or a sentence to represent plot events in lines 1 through 17. Once everyone has agreed, each should copy the summary into his or her close reader.

5. Beginning with lines that Paris and Juliet begin to speak to each other, provide the subtext for all the lines that Juliet is saying. Since she is hiding her feelings, she probably has another meaning in her head. Guess at the meaning.

6. When you have finished, complete the next steps: To Read Closely and Perform.

Scene Summaries

Directions: Write a summary for each set of lines. Examine the public, revealed emotions as well as the subtext of private, hidden emotions.

Lines 1–5 "On Thursday, sir" to "I like it not."	

Lines 6–17 "Immoderately" to "toward my cell."	

Lines 18–19	Paris says:
"Happily . . . wife" to "That may . . . wife"	
	Juliet says (write her public meaning—what Paris thinks she means):
	What Juliet really means (write her private meaning—what she's thinking and feeling but not saying):

Lines 20–21	Paris says:
"That 'may be' . . . next" to "What must be shall be."	
	Juliet says (write her public meaning):
	What Juliet really means (write her private meaning):
	Bonus: What does the Friar's statement mean?

Lines 22–23	Paris says:
"Come you . . . father?" to "To answer . . . you."	Juliet says (write her public meaning):
	What Juliet really means (write her private meaning):

Lines 24–25	Paris says:
"Do not . . . me." to "I will . . . him."	Juliet says (write her public meaning):
	What Juliet really means (write her private meaning):

Lines 26–28 "So . . . me." to "If I . . . your face."	Paris says:
	Juliet says (write her public meaning):
	What Juliet really means (write her private meaning):

To Read Closely and Perform: (Use a pencil for this part.)

1. Complete the Five Stresses Are All You've Got handout.

2. Return to scan the lines beginning with Paris's "Happily met . . ." to Juliet's "It may be so . . ." Mark where the stress falls on every second syllable.

3. Determine where the stresses should fall in Juliet's responses to Paris.

4. Appoint two people to read the scene aloud in a singsong manner, emphasizing any stressed words or syllables. Are there places where the stresses don't work perfectly? Do certain lines have more or less than ten syllables? Discuss why Shakespeare broke the iambic pentameter here.

5. **CHALLENGE QUESTION (OPTIONAL):** In Juliet's lines, circle key words—those on which the stresses fall. What themes do these words raise?

6. **CHALLENGE QUESTION (OPTIONAL):** If this conversation is the first extended conversation that Paris and Juliet have ever had, how would you describe their relationship? Create a topic sentence to summarize their interaction and offer supporting details using quotations and summaries of the action.

7. Discuss as a group Juliet's options. What should she choose to do after this scene?

    a. Suggest at least four options for Juliet.

    b. Whatever option Juliet chooses, it will be rushed because otherwise she will be married to a man she doesn't love in two days. How might the rush affect her final choice? What choice do you think Juliet will make? Why?

    c. Choose the option you think is the best for her, what Juliet *should* do (rather than what she might actually do).

In the space below, predict three possible outcomes from the choices Juliet might make:

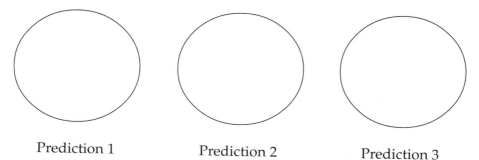

Prediction 1   Prediction 2   Prediction 3

Teaching Romeo and Juliet: *A Differentiated Approach* by Delia DeCourcy, Lyn Fairchild, and Robin Follet © 2007 NCTE.

Handout 4.b.2: Shakescholar Close Reader C

Act 4, Scene 1, Lines _____–_____

From the Friar's line "On Thursday, sir?" to Juliet's line "On Thursday next . . ."

To Read:

1. Choose a Facilitator to read these directions and keep the group on task. You will be scanning and discussing act 4, scene 1.

2. Complete the Five Stresses Are All You've Got handout.

To Discuss:

1. Scan the scene according to the rules of iambic pentameter.

2. Note where the stresses should fall in Juliet's responses to Paris in their exchange.

3. Appoint two people to read the scene aloud in a singsong manner, emphasizing any stressed words or syllables. Are there places where the stresses don't work perfectly? Do certain lines have more or less than ten syllables?

4. Discuss why Shakespeare broke the iambic pentameter here.

5. Return to act 1, scene 5. Compare the exchange between Romeo and Juliet to the exchange between Paris and Juliet. What are the main differences?

6. Juliet's line "What must be shall be" followed by Friar Laurence's line "That's a certain text" constitute a split-level line shared between Juliet and the Friar, creating one line of iambic pentameter. Why would Shakespeare use such a convention here? What is implied about character emotions and relationships here?

7. In Juliet's lines, circle key words—those on which the stresses fall. Do the same for Paris's lines. What themes do these words raise?

8. If Juliet speaks in double meanings, does that mean she is a dishonest person? Why or why not? Find a passage that illustrates her honesty or dishonesty and use it to defend or critique her.

9. How many ironic situations do you find in this scene? Name the expectations one might have of character behavior and how their actions do not meet expectations.

10. **CHALLENGE QUESTION (OPTIONAL):** If this conversation is the first extended conversation that Paris and Juliet have ever had, how would you describe their relationship? Create a topic sentence to summarize their interaction and offer supporting details using quotations and summaries of the action.

11. **CHALLENGE QUESTION (OPTIONAL):** Read to the end of the scene. Discuss as a group your beliefs about Juliet's character and how it has evolved since act 1. What qualities does she display now that she did not before?

Teaching Romeo and Juliet: *A Differentiated Approach* by Delia DeCourcy, Lyn Fairchild, and Robin Follet © 2007 NCTE.

Skill Strands

Creative Writing

Juliet's Elegy

By the end of this scene, Juliet is assumed to be dead, but we never see her funeral. Consequently, we never hear any elegies. An elegy is a speech, song, or poem offered in honor of the dead.

Assignment Option A. Write an elegy for Juliet, one that could have been spoken at her funeral. Identify who she was and who she would have been had she lived. Use words spoken by characters in the play.

Assignment Option B. Write an elegy for Juliet, one that could have been spoken at her funeral. However, assume the role of a particular character. What would the Nurse have said? Or Lord Capulet? Or Lady Capulet?

Assignment Option C. Write an elegy for Juliet, one that could have been offered at her funeral. Assuming the voice of a particular character, craft a sonnet that remains true to the personality of the character you've chosen.

Alternate Assignment. Write an elegy for yourself. Focus on who you were, who you are, and who you would have been had you not died at your current age. Ask a friend for phrases that describe you. Build those into the poem, song, or speech of tribute.

Note: See the end of act 5 for additional skill strand activities for act 4.

Name _____ Period _____

Act 4 Reading Quiz

1. Juliet threatens to do what in scene 1 when Paris has left Friar Laurence's cell?

    a. Run away from home

    b. Stab herself to death

    c. Confess to her parents her secret love for Romeo

    d. Run to Lord and Lady Montague and ask them to protect her

2. The Friar's plan is the following:

    a. Drink a potion that makes her appear as though she is dead, let herself be buried, and the Friar will dig her up and bring her to Romeo

    b. Drink a potion that makes her appear as though she is dead, let herself be laid out on a bier, and Romeo will rescue her from the vault

    c. Escape with the Nurse from her home that night and the Friar will take her to Romeo in Mantua

    d. Hold a family meeting at which the Friar says this marriage with Paris cannot occur because Juliet is no longer a virgin before marriage

3. After agreeing with the Friar on this plan, Juliet returns to her home to do what?

    a. Test the potion on the cat to see if it dies

    b. Plan her escape in the middle of the night

    c. Let the Nurse know about the plan

    d. Apologize to her father

4. When Juliet is alone in her room that night before the wedding, what worries her?

    a. The fear that the Friar might be trying to poison her

    b. The fear that Romeo has killed himself in Mantua

    c. The guilt she feels about Tybalt, that he is somewhere in heaven or hell blaming her for his death

    d. That the Nurse or Lady Capulet are spying on her

5. In scene 5, what do Lord and Lady Capulet and the Nurse discover, to their horror?

   a. Juliet's empty bed

   b. Juliet's dead body

   c. Juliet's "dead" body (she's just in a deep, comatose sleep)

   d. Romeo and Juliet in bed together

6. The following line that Juliet speaks to the Friar in scene 1—". . . this bloody knife / Shall play the umpire"—is an example of what kind of figurative language?

   a. Metaphor

   b. Simile

   c. Personification

   d. Scansion

7. When Lord Capulet says, "Death lies on her like an untimely frost / Upon the sweetest flower of the field," what two types of figurative language are at work in these lines?

   a. Simile and metaphor

   b. Metaphor and simile

   c. Simile and scansion

   d. Simile and personification

Teaching Romeo and Juliet: *A Differentiated Approach* by Delia DeCourcy, Lyn Fairchild, and Robin Follet © 2007 NCTE.

6 Act 5: Lessons, Activities, and Handouts

Act 5, Scene 1

Lesson 5.a: A Tale of Woe

Student Content and Skill Understandings

- Prepare for reading a Shakespeare text (summarize, define, predict), engage with the text (translate, analyze), and reflect (discuss, write in journal and/or outline). (AS)

- Summarize plot, identify narrative structure, and explain cause-and-effect relationships orally and in writing; predict plot outcomes based on narrative structure. (AS)

- Know features of Shakespeare's language such as blank verse, iambic pentameter, and foreshadowing. (AS)

- Scan Shakespeare's lines. (OT/ADV)

- Analyze and evaluate in writing a character's motivations, choices, and consequences according to themes. (OT/ADV)

Themes

- Students select themes that suit the act.

Materials and Handouts

- Film versions of the play directed by Franco Zeffirelli and Baz Luhrmann

Activities

STEP 1. WCA: Foreshadowing: I've Got a Bad Feeling about This! (15 minutes)

1. OPTIONAL. Journals: Ask students to respond to this prompt: Choose a theme we have studied during the play and explain why it has been the most important

theme in the play thus far. Use character choices, character personalities, setting, plot events, and any other elements that prove your point. Ask students to share aloud.

2. Review the concept of foreshadowing with students. Ask students to recall instances of foreshadowing throughout the play.

3. Explain to students that today they will seek foreshadowing and themes as they analyze act 5. Ask a student to read aloud Romeo's soliloquy through "When but love's shadows . . ." in act 5, scene 1.

STEP 2. MR and WCA: Reading Comprehension (40 minutes)

1. Ask students to work in MR pairs to translate, find foreshadowing, and track themes.

2. Back in WCA discussion, use TR questions to ask NOV students to translate lines, OT students to share evidence of foreshadowing, and ADV students to share evidence of themes.

3. Invite students to scan the lines and discuss where the stressed syllables or words fall.

4. Watch comparable scenes from either the Zeffirelli or Luhrmann version or both and ask students to comment on the cinematic texture and thematic effect such choices have.

Epilogue: Suggested Homework

Choose among the following options:

1. Students create their own close readers to show a note-taking system that has worked for them throughout the play and present their methods to the class.

2. Students complete skill strand assignments used as long-term projects (see pages 289–96).

3. Students choose essay prompts and begin gathering quotations for Quotation Sandwiches.

Notes on Differentiation

This WCA reviews and clarifies core skills taught throughout the study of the play, such as reading comprehension and note taking, analysis of narrative structure, and analysis according to theme.

Lesson 5.b: A Tale of Woe

Student Content and Skill Understandings

- Prepare for reading a Shakespeare text (summarize, define, predict), engage with the text (translate, analyze), and reflect (discuss, write in journal and/or outline). (AS)

- Summarize plot, identify narrative structure, and explain cause-and-effect relationships orally and in writing; predict plot outcomes based on narrative structure. (AS)

- Know features of Shakespeare's language such as exposition, rising action, crisis, falling action, denouement, and foreshadowing. (AS)

- Analyze and evaluate in writing a character's motivations, choices, and consequences according to themes. (OT/ADV)

Themes

- Students select themes that suit the act.

Materials and Handouts

- 5.b.1: What Is Plot? handout (a visual of Aristotle's or Freytag's plot triangle)

Activities

STEP 1. OPTIONAL. WCA: Mini-Lesson (10 minutes)

Invite a compacting student to make a presentation on Shakespeare's five-act structure based on Aristotle's definition of tragedy, or teach the mini-lesson yourself using the What Is Plot? handout. Encourage students to review as many incidents as they can remember from each act that exemplify the stages of both Aristotelian drama and Shakespeare's typical narrative thread for a tragedy.

STEP 2. TR Groups: Plotting It Out: Shakespeare's and Aristotle's Narrative Structure (30 minutes)

Ask students to form TR pairs to perform the following tasks:

1. NOV: Use the triangle structure of the five-act tragedy to plot out a key scene in the exposition, rising action, crisis, falling action, and denouement. Note: The What Is Plot? handout 5.b.1 gives strong hints through visuals about key scenes that exemplify these stages, but these designations are debatable and still need formal articulation through writing and explanation.

   a. They should create a triangle on a piece of paper and label each part of the triangle with the act and scene numbers (for example, 1.1, 2.4, etc.) that illustrate their choice for the most important scene in each act that shows true exposition, true rising action, and so forth.

   b. Then NOV students should gather quotations that justify their choice of scenes and write a Quotation Sandwich for each act.

2. OT: Decide which particular character choices in acts 1 and 2 lead to the crisis in act 3, and which particular character choices in acts 3 and 4 lead to the denouement of act 5. Create a cause-and-effect graphic (causing action → outcome). Gather quotations that justify evidence of a choice being a cause or an effect.

3. ADV: Select lines in act 5 that represent the denouement (which has the denotations of *resolution, clarification, outcome,* and *final result,* and the connotations of *untying, discovery,* and *catastrophe*). What was resolved, clarified, untied, discovered? What are the outcomes and results? What are the catastrophes? Choose one or more of these words to define the denouement in a thesis and find lines that provide evidence. Create Quotation Sandwiches that use denotation and connotation in their commentary.

STEP 3: WCA: Sharing (20 minutes)

Hear reports from the pairs in this order: NOV, OT, ADV.

Encourage students to take notes if you plan to do a larger assessment of plot events beyond the reading quiz for act 5.

Epilogue: Suggested Homework

1. At this point, students should be reading scenes independently for homework using a personalized note-taking system. Some NOV students should attempt reading larger sections, if not complete scenes, with minimal use of supplementary materials.

2. Ask students to choose questions for the upcoming Socratic seminar discussion. This discussion can be an activity that prepares students for essay writing.

3. Students can complete skill strand assignments used as long-term projects (see pages 289–96).

Notes on Differentiation

1. In the plot analysis activity, NOV students use application skills, reviewing what was already taught in the mini-lesson in order to make an analytical choice. They will also be required to provide elaborative commentary on each choice of scene, an activity that OT and ADV students have been encouraged to do on their CRs in previous acts. OT students use cause-and-effect analytical skills, and ADV students use synthesis skills. The application skill that even ADV students will struggle with is writing effective commentary on quotations. How well ADV students fare will help you gauge how much review of writing skills you should do in preparation for the upcoming essay.

2. If you would like to develop CRs or lead WCAs on other scenes in act 5, consider using Romeo's soliloquy in scene 1 beginning with "Well, Juliet, I will lie with thee tonight" until the entrance of the apothecary; Romeo's soliloquy in scene 3 after he has killed Paris that begins with, "How oft when men . . ." until his suicide; Juliet's awakening until her suicide; the Friar's speech to the gathered crowd in scene 3; and/or the Prince's final speech.

Handout 5.b.1: What Is Plot?

The definition of *plot* is "a sequence of events in which each event is the cause of another that has occurred previously." The German critic Gustav Freytag took the Greek philosopher Aristotle's classic structure and developed a diagram to help us understand how the plot of traditional narratives is organized.

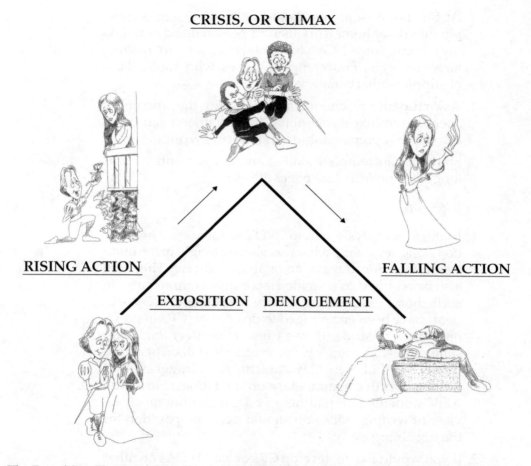

The Exposition: The exposition offers important background information on characters, plot, and setting. An important incident occurs that initiates the key conflict.

The Rising Action: The rising action illustrates more incidents that develop the conflict.

The Crisis, or Climax: The crisis or climax is the point of highest intensity in the narrative, where crucial choices are made.

The Falling Action: The falling action illustrates events that are the logical outgrowth of the crisis.

The Denouement: The denouement unknots and resolves the crisis, illustrating the consequences of the choices made.

Teaching Romeo and Juliet: *A Differentiated Approach* by Delia DeCourcy, Lyn Fairchild, and Robin Follet © 2007 NCTE.

Lesson 5.c: A Tale of Woe

Student Content and Skill Understandings

- Identify and explicate orally and in writing the reasoning for an argument using paraphrased examples and quotations from a text. (AS)
- Prewrite for an essay by gathering specific examples. (AS)

Themes

- The teacher or students select themes for Socratic discussion.

Materials and Handouts

- 5.c.1: Post-Play Poll
- 5.c.2: Essay Writing Prompts for *Romeo and Juliet* A, B, and C
- 5.c.3: Rubric for Essay Writing Prompts

Activities

STEP 1. OPTIONAL. WCA: Post-Play Poll (15 minutes)

Determine where students stand now in terms of beliefs by distributing, or asking students to take a position on, the Post-Play Poll. Whether speaking or writing, however, students should cite specific examples (paraphrased or quoted) to elaborate on their reasoning. How did character choices and plot outcomes further convince them of their original stance or change their position?

STEP 2. WCA: Review of Essay Prompts (10 minutes)

Preview the essay prompts with students and ask them to think about topics that intrigue them. If they are interested in certain prompts, they should keep their ears open during the seminar for evidence that will help them write their essays.

STEP 3. WCA, TR, or MR Groups Seminar (35–45 minutes)

Hold a Socratic seminar on questions from the play. Organize the seminar in a manner best suited to your class, using WCA, TR, or MR groups. Encourage students to make notes of evidence they hear or that others cite that is particularly compelling and that will aid essay writing, using sticky notes to mark pages in the text (NOV) or by taking notes.

Epilogue: Suggested Homework

1. Have students select, prewrite, and draft essay prompts by gathering a minimum number of quotations to prepare their essays. Dialectical journals can also be a prewriting tool.

2. Have students read and scan Romeo's speech to Juliet on her bier, searching for key themes.

3. Students can complete skill strand assignments used as long-term projects (see pages 289–96).

Notes on Differentiation

1. Consider letting students know that if they bring a certain number of quotations to class they may partner with others using the same topic to work on their essay planning; otherwise, they must work alone the following days in class to find evidence.

2. With so many essays for sale on the Internet, consider allowing several days in class for students to draft the essays so that you can more closely gauge student knowledge and skill and avoid Web and parental assistance.

Handout 5.c.1: Post-Play Poll

Directions: Decide whether you AGREE, DISAGREE, or are UNDE-CIDED about the following statements. There is no right answer for any of these questions.

1. Gregory and Sampson of the Capulet household were right to fight Abram and Balthasar to uphold their house's dignity.

   AGREE DISAGREE UNDECIDED

2. Romeo and Juliet experienced true romantic love the first night they met.

   AGREE DISAGREE UNDECIDED

3. Romeo and Juliet were right not to tell their parents about their forbidden love because it would have ended in more fighting.

   AGREE DISAGREE UNDECIDED

4. Lord Capulet should not have told Paris that Juliet would marry him without first consulting his daughter.

   AGREE DISAGREE UNDECIDED

5. Friar Laurence was right to marry Romeo and Juliet for the sake of ending the feud.

   AGREE DISAGREE UNDECIDED

6. The Nurse should not have told Juliet about her change of heart with regard to Juliet's marriage to Romeo.

   AGREE DISAGREE UNDECIDED

7. Romeo and Juliet should not have gotten married, because of the obstacles standing in their way due to the feud.

   AGREE DISAGREE UNDECIDED

8. The Nurse and Friar Laurence should be held responsible for Romeo's and Juliet's deaths.

   AGREE DISAGREE UNDECIDED

9. Romeo and Juliet had alternatives to suicide by the play's end.

    AGREE   DISAGREE   UNDECIDED

10. Mercutio made the right choice to stand up for Romeo when Romeo would not face Benvolio in a duel.

    AGREE   DISAGREE   UNDECIDED

Handout 5.c.2: Essay Writing Prompts
for *Romeo and Juliet* A

Character Explanation: A Personality Profile for a Magazine

Essay Question: Who is Romeo? Who is Juliet? The readers want to know.

Your Role: You are a reporter for *People* magazine, writing a celebrity profile after having closely observed the behavior of Romeo or Juliet. Pick one of these two protagonists and identify the three most important aspects of his or her personality.

Your Task: Identify and discuss three key personality traits, or aspects, of either character.

Mode of Discourse: Analytical-expository

Audience: Readers of *People* magazine (high school–age readers and older)

Essay Structure: Follow these guidelines to draft a good article:

- Paragraph 1, YOUR THESIS: Identify the three most important aspects of Romeo's or Juliet's personality.

- Paragraphs 2–4, YOUR EVIDENCE AND EXPLANATION: Prove that each of these aspects of personality exists.

  - Begin each paragraph with a topic sentence that states the aspect of personality.

  - For every aspect, provide at least two if not three pieces of evidence. At least one piece of evidence must be a quotation from the play with a citation.

  - Follow all rules for the Quotation Sandwich.

  - Note: Discuss only one aspect per paragraph.

- Paragraph 5, RESTATEMENT OF YOUR THESIS: Summarize the three most important aspects of Romeo's or Juliet's personality.

Causes of a Crisis: A Report to the Police

Essay Question: What caused this crime?

Your Role: You are a crime scene investigator. Find an intense scene in the play involving violence and/or death, such as when Mercutio and Tybalt fight, or when the Capulets discover Juliet "dead" in her bed. As the crime scene investigator, you must decide, or reconstruct, what caused the crime. You will share this objective report with your police chief, who will then decide whether to press charges.

Your Task: Write a summary that reconstructs the three key causes that led to the crime.
Mode of Discourse: Analytical: cause and effect
Audience: Chief of police
Essay Structure:

- Paragraph 1, YOUR THESIS: Identify three key character actions that resulted in a crisis. Note: You do not have to accuse anyone of being a criminal, since you may find more than one person at fault. Your job is to list all probable causes but not to press the charges; that's the chief's job. See Paragraph 5.

- Paragraphs 2–4, IDENTIFYING THE CAUSES: Explain how each of these causes (actions taken by particular characters) led to the crime.

  - Begin each paragraph with a topic sentence that states one of the causes.

  - For every cause, provide at least two if not three pieces of evidence. At least one piece of evidence must be a quotation from the play with a citation.

  - Follow all rules for the Quotation Sandwich.

  - Note: Discuss only one cause per paragraph.

- Paragraph 5, RESTATEMENT OF YOUR THESIS: Summarize the key actions that caused the crisis. If you wish to recommend that one character be held more responsible than any other, you may make that recommendation, but be sure there is enough evidence.

Definition and Evaluation: Let Me Tell You What Love Is

Essay Question: What is true love?
Your Role: You are a reporter for a local news media outlet. You are covering the tragedy of two teens who found and lost love—or did not. The findings of your investigation will be published in the newspaper or online media journal under a title such as "Teens Find True Love" or "Teens Fail to Find True Love." You will defend your opinion on whether Romeo and Juliet have what it takes for a long-lasting relationship.
Your Task: Create a definition of love and evaluate Romeo and Juliet's devotion to each other. Does their love meet the criteria you established?
Mode of Discourse: Evaluative

Audience: Readers of local newspapers (high school–age readers and older)

Essay Structure:

- Paragraph 1, YOUR THESIS: Define true love by identifying at least three aspects of love that a couple must demonstrate.

- Paragraphs 2–4, EVALUATION: Explain how each of these aspects are or are not demonstrated by Romeo and Juliet as a couple.

  - Begin each paragraph with a topic sentence that states one aspect of true love.

  - For every aspect, provide at least two if not three pieces of evidence. At least one piece of evidence must be a quotation from the play with a citation.

  - Follow all rules for the Quotation Sandwich.

  - Note: Discuss one aspect per paragraph. You may also include extra examples, such as those from personal experience, current events, or pop culture and its celebrities (as illustrated though movies, electronic media, and periodicals).

- Paragraph 5, RESTATEMENT OF THESIS: Summarize the aspects of true love that Romeo and Juliet did or did not demonstrate.

Definition and Evaluation: True Friendship

Essay Question: What is a true friend?

Your Role: You are a reporter for a teen magazine, writing a column for teens who have come to you needing friendship advice. Your column will be titled "10 Ways to Know If S/he's a Lifelong Friend."

Your Task: Create a definition of friendship and evaluate Romeo and Mercutio's or Romeo and Benvolio's friendship with each other. Does their friendship meet the criteria you established?

Mode of Discourse: Evaluative

Audience: Readers of local newspapers (high school–age readers and older)

Essay Structure:

- Paragraph 1, YOUR THESIS: Define true friendship by identifying at least three aspects of friendship that two friends must demonstrate.

- Paragraphs 2–4, EVALUATION: Explain how each of these aspects are or are not demonstrated by Romeo and Mercutio or Romeo and Benvolio as friends.

  - ◆ Begin each paragraph with a topic sentence that states one of the aspects of true friendship.

  - ◆ For every aspect, provide at least two if not three pieces of evidence. At least one piece of evidence must be a quotation from the play with a citation.

  - ◆ Follow all rules for the Quotation Sandwich.

  - ◆ Note: Discuss one aspect per paragraph. You may also include extra examples, such as those from personal experience, current events, or pop culture and its celebrities (as illustrated though movies, electronic media, and periodicals).

- Paragraph 5, RESTATEMENT OF THESIS: Summarize the aspects of true friendship that Romeo and Mercutio or Romeo and Benvolio did or did not demonstrate.

Teaching Romeo and Juliet: *A Differentiated Approach* by Delia DeCourcy, Lyn Fairchild, and Robin Follet © 2007 NCTE.

Handout 5.c.2: Essay Writing Prompts
for *Romeo and Juliet* B

Informational/Expository: Who Are You?

Essay Question: Who is Romeo? Who is Juliet?

Your Role: Write a psychiatrist's report after having studied the behavior of either Romeo or Juliet—unbeknownst to him or her—throughout the play.

Your Task: Pick one of these two protagonists and identify the most important factors of his or her personality.

Essay Structure:

- Paragraph 1, YOUR THESIS: Draft a thesis statement that identifies the key personality traits of either Romeo or Juliet.

- Paragraphs 2–4, IDENTIFICATION: Identify at least three characteristics of his or her personality. Focus on one characteristic per paragraph. For each characteristic, provide two examples from the play that illustrate that characteristic.

- Paragraph 5, CONCLUSION: Summarize the aspects of the character's personality.

Cause and Effect: Vengeance

Essay Question: Why do certain characters seek revenge?

Your Task: Write an essay that clearly explains why Romeo or Tybalt seeks revenge and how he goes about doing it. Finally, discuss the kind of force and repercussions his revenge has.

Essay Structure:

- Paragraph 1, THE THESIS: Draft a thesis statement that identifies the cause and effect of Romeo's or Tybalt's desire for revenge.

- Paragraph 2, CAUSES: Identify at least three causes of Romeo's or Tybalt's desire for revenge.

- Paragraph 3, CHOICES: Identify the choices that Romeo or Tybalt makes.

- Paragraph 4, RESULTS: Identify the consequences of these choices.

- Paragraph 5, CONCLUSION: Summarize the causes, choices, and results for the chosen character's revenge.

Challenge Version: Write the preceding essay but comparing Romeo to Tybalt in their desires, choices, and consequences. Evaluate whether one of them is more justified.

Analysis: Fate

Essay Question: Is fate responsible?

Your Task: The Elizabethans regarded stars and the heavens as important factors in determining the path a life would take. Shakespeare reflects this belief in his recurring references to stars, the heavens, fate, chance happenings, and fortune. Search through the play to find as many references as possible to these subjects. List citations and write commentary for each citation explaining what is happening in the play and how the characters believe that happenings in their lives are caused by fate.

Essay Structure:

- Paragraph 1, THESIS: State whether, in your opinion, one character from the play either accepts fate or fights against it.

- Paragraph 2, EVIDENCE and COMMENTARY #1: Identify one specific reference to a fate-related object or happening, preferably from acts 1 or 2. Comment on how the character from the thesis interprets the object or happening.

- Paragraph 3, EVIDENCE and COMMENTARY #2: Identify a second reference to a fate-related object or happening, preferably from acts 3 or 4. Comment on how the character from the thesis interprets the object or happening.

- Paragraph 4, EVIDENCE and COMMENTARY #3: Identify a third reference to a fate-related object or happening, preferably from acts 4 or 5. Comment on how the character from the thesis interprets the object or happening.

- Paragraph 5, IMPLICATIONS: Identify how the interpretation of the character mentioned in the thesis affects his or her subsequent actions.

- Paragraph 6, CONCLUSION: Summarize the evidence, commentary, and implications.

Evaluation: Judgment of a Tragedy

Essay Question: Who is to blame?

Your Task: Review all the most intense moments of the play and investigate how the action boiled over to this crisis moment. You are the judge reconstructing the action of the play that led to two deaths, Romeo's and Juliet's. Your evaluation will determine whether someone will be investigated or arrested.

Essay Structure:

- Paragraph 1, THESIS: Identify three people involved in a chain of decisions that leads to a tragedy. Name the person most responsible for the tragedy.

- Paragraph 2, KEY ACTIONS: Identify the key actions people choose, one after the other, that result in the tragedy.

- Paragraph 3, CRISIS MOMENTS: Determine how each of these actions leads to a crisis moment or perhaps even a crime.

- Paragraph 4, THE SCALE: Create a scale of blame: Whose actions are most culpable? Whose are least culpable? (For example, first-, second-, and third-degree murder, based on premeditation or accidental circumstances.)

- Paragraph 5, CONCLUSION: Summarize the key actions, crisis moments, and the scale; name the person who is most blameworthy.

Teaching Romeo and Juliet: *A Differentiated Approach* by Delia DeCourcy, Lyn Fairchild, and Robin Follet © 2007 NCTE.

Handout: 5.c.2: Essay Writing Prompts
for *Romeo and Juliet* C

Literary Analysis: Good and Bad

Essay Question: Can good lead to bad? Can bad lead to good?
Your Task:

> Virtue itself turns vice, being misapplied,
> And vice sometime's by action dignified.
> Within the infant rind of this weak flower
> Poison hath residence, and medicine power:

Friar Laurence's soliloquy in act 2, scene 3 discusses how good can become evil when it is badly used, and evil can sometimes be made good by the right action. Provide three clear examples of evil turning to good or good turning to evil in the play and explain how this transformation affects the turn of events.

Cause and Effect: Motifs

Essay Question: How do motifs intersect and complement one another to produce a thematic message? For example, how do books and nature combine? How do masks and space run parallel?
Your Task: Pick two significant motifs in *Romeo and Juliet*. Identify the thematic meanings they contain at the beginning of the play. Identify the thematic meanings of those same motifs at the end of the play. Discuss how and why the meanings have changed.

Argumentation: Tragedy or Comedy?

Essay Question: How is *Romeo and Juliet* both a tragedy and a comedy?
Your Task: Joseph Campbell writes in his famous work, *The Hero with a Thousand Faces*:

> Tragedy is the shattering of the forms and of our attachment to the forms; comedy, the wild and careless, inexhaustible joy of life invincible. Thus the two are the terms of a single mythological theme and experience which includes them both and which they bound: the down-going and the up-coming (*kathados* and *anodos*), which together constitute the totality of the revelation that is life, and which the individual must know and love if he is to be purged (*katharsis* = *purgatorio*) of the contagion of sin (disobedience to the di-

vine will) and death (identification with the mortal form). (Campbell, 28)

Discuss how the play parallels Campbell's thesis.

Critique: You Could Have Done This Better

Essay Question: Where has Shakespeare succeeded? Where has he failed? *Your Task*: Pick one segment of the play—the characterization of women, for example, or the portrayal of platonic love. Identify and explain Shakespeare's successes in these portrayals; identify and explain the Bard's failures, in your opinion. **CHALLENGE:** After identifying the less successful depictions, research Elizabethan culture, beliefs, and attitudes. Has Shakespeare simply portrayed the sixteenth-century vision, or has he failed in his mission as a playwright?

Argumentation: Juliet—Medieval or Modern?

Essay Question: Is Juliet empowered or disempowered by the end of the play?
Your Task: Argue that Juliet has made bold, independent choices throughout the play or that she is forced into all her choices—or both.

Literary Analysis: Public v. Private

Essay Question: Shakespeare invites us into two types of places—the lovers' private world and Verona's public spaces. How would you characterize the private places in this play versus the public?
Your Task: Dissect the elements of each space and compare and contrast such elements.

Handout 5.c.3: Rubric for Essay Writing Prompts

CRITERIA	DEVELOPING	COMPETENT	SOPHISTICATED
Content: the goal and purpose of writing; its main points and supporting details	The content ▪ identifies some aspects of the subject but neglects others ▪ includes less than two examples per aspect; some fit and some do not ▪ includes very few quotations or does not appropriately paraphrase examples ▪ provides little context or commentary for each example ▪ does not keep audience in mind	The content ▪ identifies at least three aspects of the subject ▪ includes two or more examples per aspect ▪ includes some quotations and paraphrased examples; some are appropriate and some are tangential or do not fit ▪ provides some context and commentary for each example ▪ keeps audience in mind	The content ▪ explains all three aspects of the subject thoroughly and shares thoughtful ideas that surprise the reader ▪ includes three or more well-selected quotations and paraphrased examples as supporting details ▪ provides clarifying context and elaborative commentary for each example ▪ keeps audience in mind at all times
Structure: the organization of the essay's argument	The structure ▪ breaks from the five paragraph model without reason ▪ hints at a possible thesis statement, though the thought is not complete ▪ has very few topic sentences or none at all ▪ includes details that repeat, overlap, or go astray	The structure ▪ follows the five paragraph model ▪ establishes a thesis from the beginning that previews some of the aspects but may be too general or too specific ▪ follows a clear plan established by the thesis while sometimes including unnecessary details ▪ provides topic sentences in some paragraphs	The structure ▪ follows the five paragraph model, or breaks from the model with good reason ▪ establishes a thesis from the beginning that previews all of the aspects discussed in the essay ▪ follows a clear argument or plan ▪ guides paragraphs with topic sentences

Diction: word choice and usage	The writing ■ uses a limited range of vocabulary below grade level ■ overuses adverbs and adjectives instead of concrete details, or uses a limited and general range of adjectives and adverbs ■ relies on repeated, general verbs rather than active verbs	The writing ■ uses vocabulary near grade level ■ uses effective adjectives and adverbs in conjunction with concrete details ■ uses active verbs on occasion	The writing ■ uses vocabulary at grade level that is appropriate to the topic; new words are sometimes used ■ balances concrete details that build effective images with timely use of adjectives and adverbs where commentary and generalization is needed ■ uses power verbs
Grammar & Mechanics: Grammar: system, rules, and structural relationships of language **Mechanics:** technical aspects of prose style such as punctuation	The writing suffers from several mechanical errors, including: ■ fragments ■ run-ons ■ comma splices and other comma errors ■ semicolon and colon errors ■ misspellings	The writing generally avoids: ■ fragments ■ run-ons ■ comma splices and other comma errors ■ semicolon and colon errors ■ misspellings	The writing avoids: ■ fragments ■ run-ons ■ comma splices and other comma errors ■ semicolon and colon errors ■ misspellings

Teaching Romeo and Juliet: *A Differentiated Approach* by Delia DeCourcy, Lyn Fairchild, and Robin Follet © 2007 NCTE.

Lesson 5.d: A Tale of Woe

Student Content and Skill Understandings

- Identify and explicate orally and in writing the reasoning for an argument using paraphrased examples and quotations from a text. (AS)

- Prewrite and plan for an essay. (AS)

Themes

- The teacher or students select themes for Socratic discussion.

Materials

- 5.c.2: Essay Writing Prompts A, B, and C (see pages 273–81)

- 5.c.3: Rubric for Essay Writing Prompts

- 5.d.1: Final Play Survey

Activities

STEP 1. OPTIONAL. WCA: Mini-Lesson on the Quotation Sandwich (15 minutes)

Review skills for building a coherent argument by reviewing the elements of the Quotation Sandwich (see 1.d.3: Shakescholar Close Reader, Scene 4 on pages 108–18). Explain how the topic sentence, quotation, and commentary of a paragraph on one piece of evidence can be replicated multiple times to make a larger essay. Explain a new term, *context*, the explication needed to introduce or close a quotation, by which the writer accomplishes one or more goals: (a) provides the location of the event within the plot structure and scene; (b) transitions into a quotation with such dialogue tags as "When Romeo says . . ." and so forth; and (c) offers page numbers or parenthetical citations, depending on whether your school uses MLA format. Note to students that without this information, the quotation carries no weight or power as evidence; an analogy would be if an attorney placed evidence bags in front of a jury and didn't say where this evidence came from or why it is relevant to the trial.

STEP 2. TR Groups: Prewriting and Drafting the Essay (30 minutes)

1. Once students have selected essay prompts, place students in TR groups that are further differentiated by essay prompt selected. Students can work collaboratively if they have a "ticket"—i.e., a prompt chosen and at least two pieces of evidence selected for their prewriting; otherwise, they should begin with silent work.

2. Work with groups as needed providing skill-based mini-lessons on topic sentences and thesis, quotations versus paraphrased examples, and context and commentary, or hold student conferences, alternating among NOV, OT, and ADV.

3. Repeat this lesson plan for as many days as needed, using the following strategies to change pace:

   a. Show the movie(s) while you conference with students, including those for whom the curriculum has been compacted.

   b. Ask for students to share thesis statements and three core pieces of evidence at the end of each class period.

   c. Give the Final Play Survey and have a mini-Socratic discussion afterward.

   d. Schedule presentations by compacting students.

Epilogue: Suggested Homework

Assign skill strand activities (found at the end of the chapter) as projects if students are drafting essays in class.

Notes on Differentiation

1. Assigning skill strand (interest-based) projects while students are also writing essays is a good balance for students, particularly those whose skills are NOV in writing, so that these students can experience success and pursue interests.

2. Compacting students should be finalizing projects and completing ADV essays (C prompt) if they have not written any essays during their compacting schedule.

Name_____ Period_____

Final Play Survey

This assessment is an opportunity for you to show me what you have
learned. Please make your best effort on the questions by being thorough and detailed in your responses.

You may use your copy of the play as well as any notes you have
taken in class or at home. You may use dictionaries or glossaries available in the classroom.

Please paraphrase the following lines into modern English. You
do not need to translate word for word.

Context: Romeo is in the tomb speaking to the still form of Juliet, whom
he thinks is dead. From act 5, scene 3, lines 52–59:

Text	Theme

. . . O here

_____

Will I set up my everlasting rest,

_____

And shake the yoke of inauspicious stars

_____

From this world-wearied flesh. Eyes, look your last!

_____

Arms, take your last embrace! and lips, O you

_____

The doors of breath, seal with a righteous kiss

_____

A dateless bargain to engrossing Death!

_____

Text	Theme
Come, bitter conduct, come, unsavoury guide!	
Thou desperate pilot, now at once run on	
The dashing rocks thy seasick weary bark!	
Here's to my love! [*Drinks*] O true apothecary!	
Thy drugs are quick. Thus with a kiss I die. [*Dies*]	

Themes: Reread the preceding passage. Indicate what theme or themes are evident in the lines by noting each theme next to the lines in which it appears. Then list two key themes of the play and give examples of each theme from any acts of the play.

THEME 1 _____

Examples (a paraphrase or a quotation)

a.   (from this passage)

b.   (from a related passage elsewhere in the play)

THEME 2 _____

Examples (a paraphrase or a quotation)

a.   (from this passage)

b.   (from a related passage elsewhere in the play)

Which characters best represent each of these themes? Why?

THEME 1

THEME 2

Characterization: Characterize the following characters using the following table.

Character	Adjectives to Describe Character	Examples from Play to Support Characterization
Romeo		
Juliet		

List new literary terms and devices you have learned in your study of the play and give their definitions.

Teaching Romeo and Juliet: *A Differentiated Approach* by Delia DeCourcy, Lyn Fairchild, and Robin Follet © 2007 NCTE.

Skill Strands

Creative Writing

The Abstract Nouns Are Walking Around

In act 5, scene 3, Romeo describes death as if it were human. Juliet's husband says, "Shall I believe / That unsubstantial death is amorous, / And that the lean abhorred monster keeps / Thee here in dark to be his paramour?" For this assignment, you will echo Romeo's speech. You will describe an abstract idea as if it were a creature. This type of figurative language is known as anthropomorphism, which means human qualities are given to **inanimate** objects, animals, or natural **phenomena**. If Romeo had made Death into a person, this would be known as personification. You can choose either method. To do so, please follow these steps:

1. Identify five abstract nouns: *freedom* and *love* are two examples.

2. Choose one of the nouns. Brainstorm the type of creature or person the noun would be. Male or female? Short or tall? Beautiful or ugly? Old or young? What kind of clothes would it wear? What television shows would it watch? What books would it read?

3. Describe the place where this noun would live. How would it travel? Where would it work? Who would be its friends?

4. From your brainstorming, craft a paragraph that's built on details and description. Or write a monologue from the perspective of this abstract noun.

Cinema

Which Ending?

The films' endings are significantly different. The Friar doesn't even show up in Luhrmann's ending. Juliet's suicide weapon is different in the two films. The presence of Paris, Romeo's insane behavior, the location of the twin suicides—it's all different! Write a film review in which you make your feelings known about the differences in these two endings. Which ending do you prefer? Why? Is Luhrmann's more effective visually or is it **blasphemy** that he veered so far from the Shakespeare text? What is powerful or difficult to believe about the Zeffirelli ending in the Capulet funeral vault? Make a compelling argument for the superiority of one ending over the other.

Glossary:
blasphemy: lack of respect for God, religion, and/or sacred items; cursing or irreverent comments
inanimate: not having life—the qualities of perception and will
phenomena: observable fact or event, as in nature (lightning, clouds, etc.)

Shakespeare on the Fashion Runway

You have been appointed costume designer for the next film version of *Romeo and Juliet*. You must develop a full creative concept for the film's wardrobe, including images and fabric swatches that convey the mood of the clothes for this film. You pick the time period and then start designing! You have two choices:

1. Create a presentation board with the fabric swatches and mood images, plus (pick one option) (a) drawings of one costume each for Juliet, Romeo, the Friar, the Nurse, Lord Capulet, the Prince, Mercutio, and the Apothecary; or (b) a series of drawings with several costumes for one character. Indicate clearly the scenes in which each costume appears.
2. After creating a poster with your general design concept, stage a live fashion show starring these characters. Impress the judges: the film's director and artistic director.

The Romeo and Juliet Sound Track

You have been appointed music supervisor of the new film version of *Romeo and Juliet*. And guess what? You get to pick or create the film's musical flavor. Are you an expert on rap, jazz, classical, indy rock, country music? Whatever your listening pleasure is, use that knowledge to design the sound track for this upcoming feature film.

Did you know that *theme* is also a musical term? It is the principal melody upon which variations can be created. And often the music that accompanies your favorite films and TV shows uses lyrics and musical structure to represent the ideas, motifs, and moods of those narratives.

1. Select the twelve scenes you wish to highlight in the sound track or twelve "aspects" of the play you wish to highlight. Will you pick characters, plot events, or motifs that get their own song? For example, "Romeo's Song" or "Light v. Dark" might be songs you create or song titles that you find music to match.

2. Select or create a song for each scene.

3. Create an inventive cover design that captures the musical themes and flavor of your sound track.

4. Create a song list with the artists and song titles for the back cover.

5. Write the album notes for the inside cover. Explain why you selected the song you did for each scene. How is the song relevant to what might be happening on screen?

6. Burn the CD and decorate the unburned side. Don't forget to include your name, the film's name, and some cool art on the actual CD and on the inside of the CD cover.

Socratic Discussion

Love and Marriage: **Play-Related Questions**

- How are the parental figures of the Nurse and the Friar responsible for the teenagers' deaths, if at all? Consider the job of a parent and the meaning of parental/familial love.

- How are Lady and Lord Capulet and Lady and Lord Montague responsible—or not?

Love and Marriage: **Relevance Questions**

- Is death the ultimate sacrifice for love? Discuss this idea versus the notion that suicide is an extremely selfish act.

Rebellion: **Play-Related Questions**

- Did Romeo and Juliet have other options besides ending their lives? If so, what were they? Why didn't they see those as possible options?

Chapter 6

Rebellion: **Relevance Questions**

- When they feel stuck in a tough situation, why do people often have trouble seeing alternative options? Think of a time or situation when you had such tunnel vision but that you now see other ways to deal with. What created the blinders you had on? What other characters in literature, film, and visual art have been portrayed in similar situations?

Fate: **Play-Related Questions**

- Romeo decides to defy the stars to be with his love, Juliet, in heaven. Is it possible for him to defy the stars if they are the force he has believed in and been guided by throughout the play? Examine this conundrum.

Fate: **Relevance Questions**

- How does one balance a belief in fate with a belief in personal responsibility? Is this possible?

Dichotomy and Paradox: **Play-Related Questions**

- The lovers' suicides put an end to the feud. How does good come from this tragedy?

Dichotomy and Paradox: **Relevance Questions**

- Consider how good has come from tragedy in your life as well as in historical and current events. How is such a transformation possible?

Identity: **Play-Related Questions**

- Romeo's and Juliet's identities are largely determined by their family names. How is their double suicide a product of their identities?

Identity: **Relevance Questions**

- How do social rules affect the identities of individuals in modern society?

Motifs: Play-Related Questions

- *Time: haste v. slowness*: Over what stretch of time does the play take place? How does this affect the nature of the events and the decisions made? How does this speed affect us as readers/viewers?

Motifs: Relevance Questions

- *Time: haste v. slowness*: How does the compression of events tend to affect you and your judgment? How do you slow life down when it seems to be in overdrive and moving at warp speed? Does life move too quickly or too slowly for you?

Name_____ Period_____

Act 5 Reading Quiz

1. What does the servant Balthasar bring to Romeo in scene 1?

    a. The news that Juliet is waiting for him in a coma

    b. A letter from Friar Laurence

    c. A letter from his parents, Lord and Lady Montague

    d. The news that Juliet is dead

2. What does Romeo decide to do after Balthasar leaves?

    a. Find a secret way to visit Juliet in the hospital

    b. Purchase a poison from an apothecary

    c. Ignore his parents' letter

    d. Kill himself immediately while he is in Mantua

3. What news does Friar John bring to Friar Laurence that causes him to respond, "Unhappy fortune!"

    a. He could not visit Romeo in Mantua with a letter explaining that Juliet is not really dead.

    b. He could not convince the Capulets and Montagues to forget their feud.

    c. He has just heard that Romeo killed himself.

    d. He has just been to the hospital to see Juliet and found her dead.

4. Paris brings flowers to Juliet's tomb and sees Romeo there. What does he think Romeo is there to do?

    a. Profane a Capulet body since Romeo is a Montague and has killed Tybalt

    b. Steal Juliet's body

    c. Kill Paris

    d. Meet with the Capulets and explain everything

5. What happens after Paris and Romeo argue?

    a. Paris leaves to get help.

    b. They fight and Romeo kills Paris.

    c. The Friar appears and stops their fighting.

  d. Paris kills Romeo.

6. When Romeo sees Juliet, what choice does he eventually make?

  a. To take her body back with him to Mantua for a proper burial

  b. To wait for the Friar so he can get an explanation

  c. To kill himself

  d. To confront the Capulets for trying to force Juliet to marry Paris

7. What happens next?

  a. The Friar arrives and makes Romeo leave before he is caught by the night watch; Juliet wakes up, loses her mind as she feared at being trapped in a vault with dead bodies, and kills herself; Romeo comes back, sees her bleeding to death, and kills himself.

  b. The Friar arrives; Juliet awakens from her coma and sees Romeo dead; the Friar tries to make her leave before the night watch comes, but she will not, and she stabs herself with a dagger.

  c. Paris and Romeo beg Juliet to choose between them; they fight; Paris kills Romeo; Juliet tells Paris she can never love him; Juliet falls upon a sword.

  d. The Montagues and Capulets arrive, making accusations at both Romeo and Juliet, and Romeo and Juliet escape, only to be killed by the night watch.

8. After the lovers have died, who explains what has happened?

  a. Friar John

  b. The Nurse

  c. Paris

  d. Friar Laurence

9. Who declares, "See what a scourge is laid upon your hate, / That heaven finds means to kill your joys with love!"

  a. The Prince

  b. Lord Montague

       c. Lord Capulet

       d. The Nurse

10. What do the Montagues and Capulets decide to do?

       a. Serve a jail sentence

       b. Raise statues to honor each other's children

       c. Go into business together

       d. Banish themselves from Verona

Appendix A: Grading in a Differentiated Classroom: Measure for measure

How you grade depends on many elements, such as your school, district (if applicable), and state or standardized tests' criteria. Therefore we recommend the following approach to handling grading of student work.

Consult with colleagues, then department chairs, then principal(s) or head of school in the appropriate hierarchy before implementing your grading system. It is crucial that you gain support for your methods before any questions arise from students or parents.

Identify certain assessments (such as final play surveys, reading quizzes, and essays) as standardized assessments for the unit. Like state or national tests, these assessments represent grade-level expectation. All students will be graded by a standard letter grade A through F rubric or whatever standard your school uses. The advantage to this method is that you have a grade-level, "at standard" measure of each student. The drawback to this method is that your NOV students could be earning Ds and Fs despite progress they make during the unit, and your ADV students could make easy As. However, this is the traditional NOV and ADV experience, with the OT students floating somewhere in the middle.

Identify certain assessments (such as CRs and MR group activities like dramatic performance) as differentiated assessments. You can use differentiated rubrics to grade these, so that an NOV student's work on a close reader is assessed by a rubric gauging those skills expected of an NOV student, while an OT or ADV student's work is assessed by a rubric gauging those skills expected of an OT or ADV student. For CR activities, your NOV students will be asked more knowledge and comprehension questions and fewer analysis, synthesis, and evaluation questions since your emphasis is on comprehension. In your grade book, mark the appropriate column with a special designation such as a "D" for differentiated, and then give the grade that you find appropriate to each student's readiness level based on the relevant rubric. The advantage to this method is that your NOV students who are reading at their readiness level or pursuing an interest don't always make low grades, and your ADV students don't always make high grades. The drawback to this method is that students or parents might perceive this system as unfair because not all assessments are standardized, even though students don't arrive in your classroom in one-size-fits-all formats. Here is where your department chair and administration must support you wholeheartedly in this venture. You should work with administrators to craft a standard explanation and justification of differentiated instruction and how it benefits student learning. Feel free to use our philosophical statements on page 1.

A tip for paper management: Decide which assignments need rubrics and which do not. Do not grade everything. To pace grading, collect one-third of the NOV, OT, and ADV work on a regular basis so you get a sense of the various readiness levels in your class. Alternate between skimming for diagnostic information and in-depth evaluation. For example, basic reading comprehension questions can earn straight points (5/5 for basic effort), while Quotation Sandwiches can be graded more rigorously with a 10/10 scale. Articulate to students the differences you make between the scores. In the course of this unit, you will be able to collect each student's homework multiple times. You can also ask students to choose their best close reader, best journal, best creative writing skill strand assignment, and so forth from each act and grade just that work as representative. To demonstrate your expectations for future students, save models of the best NOV, best OT, and best ADV assignments that students complete and use these as anonymous samples.

Appendix B: The Best of the Bard on the Web: All the Web's a stage

The seemingly endless number of Internet websites about Shakespeare shows that the study of Shakespeare is thriving in our society. Following is a list of what we feel are the best places to begin. These sites are professional, updated, reliable, and, most important, relevant to teaching and your classroom. Happy surfing!

About.com
<http://shakespeare.about.com/>

> Perhaps the most extensive site for the literary study of Shakespeare, including discussions and close readings of key soliloquies, an Elizabethan glossary, a quotation collection organized by theme, and, of course, plenty of history resources. The site is frequently updated.

Charles and Mary Lamb: Tales from Shakespeare
<http://shakespeare.palomar.edu/lambtales/LAMBTALE.HTM>

> The famous sibling duo provides elegant plot summaries of Shakespeare's plays as short stories.

Connotations: A Journal for Critical Debate
<http://www.uni-tuebingen.de/connotations/index.html>

> This site hosts an international journal of literary criticism with a forum for discussion of its criticism and articles.

Encyclopaedia Britannica's Guide to Shakespeare
<http://search.eb.com/shakespeare/index2.html>

> Encyclopaedia Brittanica's extensive and beautifully designed site that includes the history of Shakespeare and other writers of his day, the Globe Theatre, the Elizabethan context, and of course the text of all his plays. In addition, thumbnail sketches of characters from all the plays are included, along with relevant maps, Shakespeare quizzes, a filmography, and other historical information related to modern productions of the Bard's work.

Folger Shakespeare Library
<http://www.folger.edu/index.cfm>

> A veteran in the art of teaching Shakespeare, the Folger Library provides an extensive section for teachers, including lesson plan archives with lessons created and tested by classroom teachers.

In Search of Shakespeare
<http://www.pbs.org/shakespeare>

> In cooperation with the Folger Library, the Corporation for Public Broadcasting offers lesson plans and a number of other resources relating to Shakespeare.

Interactive Shakespeare Project
<http://www.holycross.edu/departments/theatre/projects/isp/>

> A collaboration between the College of the Holy Cross English and theater departments, this site offers wonderful teaching ideas, including the use of video and performance in the classroom and a virtual tour of the Globe Theatre.

Mainely Shakespeare
<http://www.mainelyshakespeare.com/>

> This website is "dedicated to the teaching of Shakespeare through the performing arts."

Mr. William Shakespeare and the Internet
<http://shakespeare.palomar.edu/>

> For both teachers and students, this comprehensive site is populated with historical information, lessons, and links.

No Sweat Shakespeare
<http://www.nosweatshakespeare.com/shakespeare_dictionary.htm>

> This site, with e-book prose versions of Shakespeare texts, is available for a fee. The site also provides lesson ideas, quotations, and other resources. This site is a possibility for students who need supplementary reading of the narrative to provide transitions and deeper comprehension.

Royal Shakespeare Company
<http://www.rsc.org.uk/home/default.asp>

> The Royal Shakespeare Company's exhaustive website on Shake-

speare's works and life, including a Learning section with play summaries, guides, pictures, and exhibitions, as well as a discussion of the authorship debate. Of course, they also highlight their upcoming productions.

Shakespeare: Subject to Change
http://www.ciconline.org/shakespeare

Cable in the Classroom created this multimedia website that includes interactive lessons on the printing process of the Bard's plays as well as variations in the performances of his work. Created in conjunction with the editor of *Shakespeare Magazine*, the Huntington Library, and the Folger Library, it is a reliable and eye-catching site.

Shakespearean Tragedy by A. C. Bradley
<http://www.clicknotes.com/bradley/>
Bradley's lectures on tragedy are available online.

Shakespeare Illustrated
<http://shakespeare.emory.edu/illustrated_index.cfm>

This Emory University website, "a work in progress, explores nineteenth-century paintings, criticism and productions of Shakespeare's plays and their influences on one another."

Shakespeare Resource Center
<http://www.bardweb.net/about.html>

This site is an extensive resource for Shakespearean and Elizabethan history, information on the Globe Theatre, and plenty of excellent links to other websites, especially those about Shakespeare's language. The site is well organized and informative.

Shakespeare's Globe
<http://www.shakespeares-globe.org/>

This is the website of the rebuilt Globe Theatre in Bankside, London.

Appendix C: Suggested Readings: O let my books be then the eloquence

Adler, Mortimer J., et al. *The Paideia Proposal: An Educational Manifesto*. New York: Macmillan, 1982.

Benjamin, Amy. *Differentiated Instruction: A Guide for Middle and High School Teachers*. Larchmont, New York: Eye on Education, 2002.

Bloom, Harold. "*Romeo and Juliet*." *Shakespeare: The Invention of the Human*. New York: Riverhead, 1998.

Charney, Maurice. *How to Read Shakespeare*. New York: Peter Lang, 1992.

Chute, Marchette. *An Introduction to Shakespeare*. New York: Dutton, 1951.

Crowther, John, ed. *Romeo and Juliet*. No Fear Shakespeare series. New York: SparkNotes, 2003.

Crystal, David, and Ben Crystal. *Shakespeare's Words: A Glossary and Language Companion*. London: Penguin, 2002.

Drapeau, Patti. *Differentiated Instruction: Making It Work*. New York: Scholastic, 2004.

Gibbons, Brian, ed. *Romeo and Juliet*. London: Arden Shakespeare, 2002.

King-Shaver, Barbara, and Alyce Hunter. *Differentiated Instruction in the English Classroom: Content, Process, Product, and Assessment*. Portsmouth, NH: Heinemann, 2003.

Kise, Jane A. G. *Differentiation through Personality Types: A Framework for Instruction, Assessment, and Classroom Management*. Thousand Oaks, CA: Corwin. 2007.

Papp, Joseph, and Elizabeth Kirkland. *Shakespeare Alive!* New York: Bantam, 1988.

Roberts, Terry. *The Paideia Seminar: Guide and Workbook*. Chapel Hill, NC: New View, 1996.

Spolin, Viola. *Theater Games for the Classroom: A Teacher's Handbook*. Evanston, IL: Northwestern UP, 1986.

Strong, Michael. *The Habit of Thought: From Socratic Seminars to Socratic Practice*. Chapel Hill, NC: New View, 1996.

Tomlinson, Carol Ann. *How to Differentiate in Mixed-Ability Classrooms*. 2nd ed. Alexandria, VA: Association for Supervision and Curriculum Development, 2001.

Tomlinson, Carol Ann, and Cindy Strickland. *Differentiation in Practice: A Resource Guide for Differentiating Curriculum, Grades 9–12.* Alexandria, VA: Association for Supervision and Curriculum Development, 2005.

Wiggins, Grant, and Jay McTighe. *Understanding by Design.* Exp. 2nd ed. Upper Saddle River, NJ: Pearson Education, 2006.

Witherell, Nancy L., and Mary C. McMackin. *Graphic Organizers and Activities for Differentiated Instruction in Reading.* New York: Scholastic, 2002.

Works Cited

Adler, Mortimer J. "How to Mark a Book." Keene State College. 5 Mar 2007 <http://academics.keene.edu/tmendham/documents/ AdlerMortimerHowToMarkABook_20060802.pdf>.

Bloom, Benjamin S. *Taxonomy of Educational Objectives: The Classification of Educational Goals*. New York: Longmans, Green, 1956.

Campbell, Joseph. *The Hero with a Thousand Faces*. New York: Princeton UP, 1949.

Charles and Mary Lamb: Tales from Shakespeare. Ed. Terry A. Gray. 1997–1998. 7 December 2006 <http://shakespeare.palomar.edu/lambtales/ LAMBTALE.HTM>.

Crispen, Kelly. "Life of Women in Tudor England" *Tudor Menu*. 15 June 2005 <http://tudors.crispen.org/tudor_women/>.

Crowther, John, ed. *Romeo and Juliet*. No Fear Shakespeare series. New York: SparkNotes, 2003.

Crystal, David, and Ben Crystal. *Shakespeare's Words: A Glossary and Language Companion*. London: Penguin, 2002.

"Describing Shots." *Media Know All*. Ed. Karina Wilson. 8 May 2005. Media Know All: A Webguide for Media Students. 30 May 2005 <http:// www.mediaknowall.com/camangles.html>.

"Directing." *Cinema: How Are Hollywood Films Made?* 2005 Annenberg Media. 30 May 2005 <http://www.learner.org/exhibits/cinema/ directing2.html>.

"Glossary of Film Terms." *The Gin Game*. 2003. PBS Hollywood Presents. 30 May 2005 <http://www.pbs.org/hollywoodpresents/gingame/ glossary.html>.

Griffin, Bill, ed. *C. W. (Bill) Griffin VCU English Department*. 15 June 2005 <http://www.people.vcu.edu/~bgriffin/>.

Hammerschmidt-Hummel, Hildegard. "The Most Important Subject That Can Possibly Be." *Connotations: A Journal for Critical Debate*. 19 August 2006 <http://www.uni-tuebingen.de/connotations/index.html>. [Type "Hildegard Hammerschmidt-Hummel" into the site search engine.]

King, Warren. *No Sweat Shakespeare*. "Shakespeare Dictionary and Translations." 2004. 7 December 2006 <http:// www.nosweatshakespeare.com/shakespeare_dictionary.htm>.

Levenson, Jill. "'*Alla Stoccado* carries it away': Codes of Violence in *Romeo and Juliet*." *Shakespeare's* Romeo and Juliet: *Texts, Contexts, and Interpretation*. Ed. Jay L. Halio. Newark: U of Delaware P, 1995. 19 August 2006 <http://www.clicknotes.com/romeo/LevensonCodes.html>.

"Masque." *Wikipedia*. 19 August 2006 <http://en.wikipedia.org/wiki/Masque>.

O'Brien, Peggy, ed. *Shakespeare Set Free: Teaching* Romeo and Juliet, Macbeth, A Midsummer Night's Dream. New York: Washington Square Press, 1993.

Papp, Joseph, and Elizabeth Kirkland. *Shakespeare Alive!* New York: Bantam, 1988.

Romeo + Juliet. Dir. Baz Luhrmann. Perf. Leonardo DiCaprio, Claire Danes. 20th Century Fox, 1996.

Romeo and Juliet. Dir. Franco Zeffirelli. Perf. Leonard Whiting, Olivia Hussey. Paramount, 1968.

Secara, Maggie Pierce. "Life in Elizabethan England." Ed. Maggie Ros. A *Compendium of Common Knowledge*. 5 Sept. 2004. 17 June 2005 <http://elizabethan.org/compendium/index.html>.

Shakespeare, William. *Romeo and Juliet*. Ed. Brian Gibbons. Oxford: Oxford UP, 2002.

Shakespeare, William. *Romeo and Juliet*. Ed. Brian Gibbons. London: Arden, 2002.

Weller, Philip. "Summary of Act I, Scene I." *Shakespeare Navigators*. 25 July 2006 <http://www.clicknotes.com/romeo/S11.html>.

Authors

Delia DeCourcy holds a BA in English with highest honors from Oberlin College and a master's degree from the Breadloaf School of English at Middlebury College. A nine-year veteran of the independent school English classroom, DeCourcy worked concurrently as an administrator, most recently as assistant head of the middle school at Cary Academy in Cary, North Carolina. Previously, she directed Summerbridge Louisville at Kentucky Country Day School, an academic enrichment program for public school students in which all teaching is performed by high school and college students. She also served as a teacher-editor for the online educational publication *MidLink Magazine*, sponsored by North Carolina State University, SAS Institute, and the University of Central Florida. DeCourcy was a 2002 recipient of a William Friday Fellowship at Cary Academy, and in 2005 her students' work was featured in *Writing Magazine* online. At work on her first novel, she is currently a student in the creative writing program at the University of Michigan in Ann Arbor, where she lives with her loyal German shepherd, Reign.

Lyn Fairchild holds a BA in English and an MA in education from Stanford University. She has taught English, creative writing, and other humanities courses in public and independent secondary schools for over thirteen years. She has also served as a gifted education resource teacher and a curriculum consultant. Currently she serves as Coordinator of Independent Learning at Duke University Talent Identification Program developing curriculum for gifted youth, including *The Writer's Journey*. Fairchild has been recognized as a Distinguished Teacher with the Presidential Scholar Program, as a 2001 recipient of the All-USA Teacher 3rd Team Award, and as a 2002 recipient of the William Friday Fellowship. She is coauthor of *The Compassionate Classroom: Lessons That Nurture Wisdom and Empathy*, and her differentiated lessons on *Macbeth* and the Civil War are featured in ASCD's *Differentiation in Practice*. She is a featured writer on *Faculty Shack*, an online magazine for teachers, and she is also working on her first novel.

Fairchild lives in Chapel Hill, North Carolina, with her husband Greg Hawks, a bluegrass musician.

Robin Follet holds a BA in English with high honors from the University of Virginia and an MA in education from the College of William and Mary. Currently the chair of the Upper School English Department at Cary Academy, he has taught a variety of courses over the past decade, ranging from world literature to creative writing. He has also been a faculty member at the West Virginia Governor's Honors Academy. In 2001, Follet was a Fulbright Exchange Teacher to Romania, where he spent a year teaching English at Colegiul National "Unirea," an award-winning high school in Focsani, Romania. That experience formed the basis for several published articles and a manuscript of collected essays.

This book was typeset in Palatino and Helvetica by Electronic Imaging.
Typefaces used on the cover were Aquinas, Berkeley, and Copperplate.
The book was printed on 50-lb. Williamsburg Offset paper by Versa Press, Inc.